CHICANO BAKES

CHICANO BAKES

Recipes for Mexican Pan Dulce, Tamales, and My Favorite Desserts

ESTEBAN CASTILLO

HARPER DESIGN

An Imprint of HarperCollinsPublishers

First published in 2022 by

Harper Design
An Imprint of HarperCollins*Publishers*
195 Broadway
New York, NY 10007
Tel: (212) 207-7000
Fax: (855) 746-6023
harperdesign@harpercollins.com
hc.com

Distributed throughout the world by
HarperCollinsPublishers
195 Broadway
New York, NY 10007

ISBN 978-0-06-314051-6

Library of Congress Control Number: 2022939856

Printed in Canada

First Printing, 2022

CONTENTS

Introduction 9

15

CHAPTER 1
The Basics

43

CHAPTER 2
Pan Dulce Mexicano
Mexican Sweet Bread

93

CHAPTER 3
Postres
Desserts

129

CHAPTER 4
Pasteles
Cakes

159

CHAPTER 5
Antojitos
Small Bites

187

CHAPTER 6
Bebidas
Drinks

Acknowledgments 214

Index 216

INTRODUCTION

For many of us, 2020 was a roller coaster. I was just starting to wrap up my first cookbook, *Chicano Eats: Recipes from My Mexican-American Kitchen*, when COVID-19 hit. I celebrated my thirtieth birthday on March 7, and at the time I felt as if I was at the top of the roller coaster's first steep climb. A week later, I was heading to Seattle for a video shoot when I realized that things were about to get pretty serious. After the plane landed, I turned my phone on to read a headline about more COVID-19-related cases being detected in Seattle. It was like the amusement park's ride attendant had suddenly pressed the "go" button a second too early y la sangre se me fue hasta los talones. I became very anxious and started worrying about what the rest of the year would look like. Long story short, the rest of 2020 would be filled with a lot of questions and stress, but most important, also a lot of learning and growing.

Chicano Eats was published in the summer of 2020, on June 30. Publishing a book geared toward someone like my younger self, who had moved away from home for the first time and missed their parents' cooking but had no idea where to start, was a dream come true, but for me the weeks leading up to its release were filled with anxiety. I was thinking to myself, *We're in the middle of a pandemic! Are people going to be able to buy it? How am I going to promote the book?* I also wondered about what recipes folks would gravitate toward first! My questions were quickly answered the first day the book was out—and I felt as if the roller coaster was back to a smooth ride.

One of the recipes that went viral overnight was my dulce de leche chocoflan. This recipe was featured in the *New York Times*'s food section, as well as other outlets like Food52. Everyone on Instagram started tagging me as soon as they made it. Folks were always amazed to see how the cake batter would go in first and then the flan on top of it, and during the baking process the batter and flan would flip places due to their density. So when the cake was inverted, the flan was now on top, and the cake on the bottom. No matter how many times I explained this tasty magic trick, folks would still ask, Shouldn't the chocolate cake be on top?

I was relieved to see that the community I had built over the past few years with my blog, *Chicano Eats*, was so excited to have a book with recipes that felt and tasted like home, a cookbook they could finally relate to, one that reimagined Mexican cuisine from a Mexican-American point of view. People who look like me don't often get the opportunity to showcase the things that matter the most to our communities—no matter how hard we work. I was also very surprised to see that although summer had just started, everyone was flocking to the desserts chapter, as well as the more time-intensive recipes like my mole coloradito, birria, and carnitas. It all made sense though, because my community loves a hot dish when temperatures begin to soar. (I'm looking at you, caldo de pollo!) As COVID-19 spread and the world continued its lockdown, people kept baking. I was constantly asked if I had a recipe for this dessert, that cookie, or this pan dulce (pan dulce is the catchall term for Mexico's pastries and sweet breads). I quickly realized that if I ever wrote another book, it would need to expand on my dessert recipes.

Since a traditional in-person book tour was out of the question due to the pandemic, I decided to launch a series of online cooking classes in the fall of 2020 so I could connect with readers from the comfort of their own homes and walk them through some of the more "difficult" recipes in the book. In those classes we made birria, pozole, flan, churros, mole, salsas, and chocoflan.

Their enthusiasm made me realize that so many people in my community wanted to join in the baking frenzy caused by the pandemic, but the resources and books for the sweets and pastries that my community wanted to bake and enjoy just weren't available—and whatever was out there just wasn't easy to make. It wasn't tried and true. This is where the idea for *Chicano Bakes* was born.

I grew up in Santa Ana (SanTana for my locals), California—a predominantly Hispanic community in Southern California—right behind a shopping center that included El Toro Meat Market, a Mexican grocery store that is very much embedded in the fiber of the community. As the saying goes,

El que no conoce El Toro, no conoce Santa Ana ("If you don't know El Toro, you don't know Santa Ana"), and I didn't realize how much of a gift that place was when I was growing up until I moved away for college. My family had daily access to a butcher for fresh cuts of meat, hot carnitas, crispy chicharrones, and dairy products, as well as fruits and veggies like cebollitas, ciruelas, caña, and nances that we just couldn't find anywhere else. Two doors down from El Toro was a Mexican bakery, and we could always tell when the panadero was bringing out fresh bread, because the sweet scent of cinnamon sugar danced through the air, like a sweet siren song inviting us in for a warm roll.

My dad would typically spend his evenings making spurs in the garage (that's a story for another day), and when we started to smell the toasted cinnamon in the air, I'd go grab him and we'd walk over for pan dulce. A fresh slice of cortadillo (Mexican pink cake) was my favorite, and a warm concha de vainilla with an ice-cold Coke was his.

Panaderías in the US vary depending on the community. In one town, a panadería might be a small shelf located inside a gas station, while in another it might be a storefront that focuses on selling fresh bread, coffee, champurrado, sweets, and cakes. In other areas, a panadería might stretch what they sell to make antojitos (savory bites).

Chicano Bakes captures my favorite traditional staple recipes from la panadería, while also giving

you the opportunity to let your hair down with the fun fusion Chicano Eats recipes that I'm known for! You're going to get conchas, empanadas, and tamales as well as cakes, cocktails, and aguas frescas.

You're also going to notice that this book looks and feels different from my first cookbook. That is totally intentional. *Chicano Eats* captured my childhood and my roots, and *Chicano Bakes* is meant to encapsulate where I am in 2022. However, although my viewpoint as an artist and photographer has changed, my approach to keeping my recipes simple, as well as tried and true, remains the same. From the versatility of the recipes in the basics chapter, to the next five chapters in which I share what I love about pan dulce mexicano (Mexican sweet bread), postres (desserts), pasteles (cakes), antojitos (small bites), and bebidas (drinks), I want this book to be useful to folks, especially to my community, who might feel intimidated by baking books that don't cater to us. And I've made sure this book is well rounded so you can get great use out of it year-round, not just during the holidays or winter months.

Taking the traditional route has never been the way I go. We've all seen the same handful of ways that you can style cakes, pies, and chocolate chip cookies, but I wanted to do something totally different. Music gets me through the workday. When I was teaching my online cooking classes and developing the recipes for this book, I had

Kylie Minogue's album *Fever* and Kacey Musgraves's *Golden Hour* on repeat, as well as lots of disco. Coming out to my dad at age thirty (another story I'll have to share with you someday) took so much weight off my shoulders and gave me a sense of freedom that I had never felt before. That feeling of happiness and euphoria is the same feeling that listening to disco gave me at the start of the pandemic. Disco fills me with cheer, makes me want to dance, and allows me to pour even more passion into whatever I'm working on.

So I closed my eyes and started listening to my work playlist, looking for sounds and textures for inspiration. Sylvester came on first, singing "You Make Me Feel (Mighty Real)," and his fun, unapologetic, and colorful queer tone danced around, painting rainbows in my head. Then came Thelma Houston with "Don't Leave Me This Way," and I just envisioned her singing her song in a firm yet delicate tone laced with glamour. And then ABBA came on singing "Gimme Gimme Gimme," and thinking of the drama of their (very bold and colorful) outfits left me entranced.

I wanted each shot to feel like portraits, so I took my favorite parts of disco—the textures, the luxe velvet fabrics, the glamour, the indulgence, the lights, the sparkle, and its joy—and infused them throughout the book. I hope you enjoy this colorful and magnetic ride you're about to embark on. Welcome to *Chicano Bakes*!

When I was thinking of what to include in a "basics" chapter, I kept in mind the many different recipes that lay the framework for the rest of the book. In this chapter, you'll find versatile recipes that have elements that we'll be using throughout *Chicano Bakes*, like corn tortillas, whose dough can also be used to make chochoyotes (corn masa dumplings) for my Crema De Frijol con Chochoyotes (page 170), or Picaditas (page 169), sopes topped with salsa. You'll find flour tortillas, whose dough can be used to make my Caramel Apple Cheesecake Empanadas (page 97), as well as recipes for teleras and bolillos, which can be used for things like tortas or Molletes (page 178). I'll also be teaching you how to make vanilla extract from scratch as well as different variations on the caramel sauce that can be used alongside many other recipes throughout the book!

THE BASICS

My Pantry

Here's a quick peek into the items in my pantry, which I always keep well stocked, and that we'll be using throughout the book.

BUTTER: Because the salt content of different brands of salted butter differs, I only use unsalted butter so I can have better control of the amount of salt in a recipe.

COCOA POWDER: I typically use Dutch process cocoa powder in my recipes, as it gives a richer color and flavor, but you can easily use natural cocoa powder in any of the recipes if you're in a pinch or can't find Dutch process cocoa at the grocery store.

CONDENSED MILK: I use sweetened condensed milk throughout the book to add a touch of creamy sweetness to many of my desserts.

DULCE DE LECHE AND CAJETA: These creamy caramelized milk-based sauces can be used as a drizzle, filling, or spread. Dulce de leche is traditionally made with cow's milk, and cajeta with goat's milk. Head over to page 41 to make dulce de leche, and page 36 to make cajeta envinada (cajeta made with a touch of rum) from scratch.

EGGS: All of the recipes in this book call for large eggs, so always double-check, as a different size could affect the outcome of the recipe. If a recipe specifies that an egg should be at room temperature and you forgot to get the egg out of the refrigerator, you can quickly warm an egg to room temperature by placing it in a small glass of warm water. Room-temperature eggs tend to mix into batters more easily when the rest of the ingredients are also at room temperature.

FLOUR: We're keeping things easy and only using unbleached all-purpose flour throughout the book.

GUAVA PASTE: Guava paste is going to show up in a few recipes, so make sure to grab seedless guava paste. If you can find the paste sold as a block, even better.

KOSHER SALT: I use Diamond Crystal brand kosher salt for all my recipes because I like the feel of it when using a pinch to salt my food. I know this brand can be difficult to find in some areas so I also give the measurement of fine sea salt in all the recipes in the book. If you're ever unsure how to convert from kosher to fine sea salt, just remember it's half the measurement by volume: 1 teaspoon Diamond Crystal kosher = ½ teaspoon fine sea salt.

LARD: Lard keeps my bolillos, flour tortillas, chochoyotes, teleras, and tamales moist and fluffy, but if you have any rendered bacon fat, use that instead for more added flavor.

LEAVENING: I keep my pantry stocked with active dry yeast, baking powder, and baking soda for cakes and breads. They each have different jobs in baked goods and are not interchangeable. Baking soda is also a great browning agent and helps give dulce de leche and cajeta a nice brown color.

MASA HARINA: We now live in a time when multiple choices for masa harina exist! Some brands may be coarser than others and require more moisture, but the brand you're most likely to find at your local grocery store is Maseca, which is what we'll be using throughout the book. Although Maseca also makes masa harina specifically for tamales, we'll only be using regular Maseca, which works for tortillas, empanadas, tamales, atoles, and sopes.

MILK AND BUTTERMILK: Milk and buttermilk not only add moisture to baked goods but also add fats. I love using buttermilk in most of my recipes because it adds a nice tang and a double dose of fat so breads, cakes, and pastries stay soft and moist.

OIL: All the recipes that call for oil will specify in the recipe which type is needed, though most likely it's going to be a neutral oil. A neutral oil adds fat and moisture without adding any flavor. The most popular options at the grocery store are canola and vegetable, but a recently more available option that I also like to use is avocado oil.

PUFF PASTRY: I like to keep a few sheets of store-bought puff pastry in the freezer for making Danishes, orejitas, and pastelitos. I like to use Pepperidge Farm brand puff pastry, as that is the brand you're most likely to run into!

SHORTENING: Mexican pastries tend to use shortening, as it's more economical. It's also shelf-stable, and it keeps baked goods moist. Butter isn't always a good substitute for shortening, as it contains moisture and isn't 100 percent fat; in some cases, it will change the texture of the recipe! To infuse baked goods with butter flavor when using shortening, opt for butter-flavored shortening, or purchase butter flavoring at your local cake supply shop.

VANILLA EXTRACT AND VANILLA PASTE: Pure vanilla extract and paste are not only important for a vanilla flavor but also help enhance other flavors as well. Always look for pure vanilla extract or paste, not imitation. If you want to cut down on its cost and make your own, see Vanilla Extract (page 38) for the full instructions.

Tools

Having the right tools is important—and not using the right tools can greatly affect the outcome of a recipe. Before you start baking from this book, make sure to get yourself a good scale and oven thermometer. My cup measurements are based on weights, so if you aren't using a scale to properly measure your ingredients, you might be packing extra flour or sugar into each cup. If you are baking in an oven that runs 15° to 20°F (8 to 11°C) hotter or cooler than it should, you are going to run into issues with things baking too quickly or not quickly enough.

BAKING SHEETS: The color of your baking sheets is important! I like to invest in light-colored baking sheets, as darker ones will conduct more heat. My favorite source for good-quality aluminum baking sheets is a local restaurant supply store. These stores are most likely used by your local bakeries, and they'll probably have the best prices.

COMAL: This is a flat, typically round skillet used to cook tortillas and things like sopes, huaraches, and gorditas. If you don't have one, a large nonstick or cast-iron skillet will work.

GLASS AND STAINLESS STEEL BOWLS: I like having a combination of small glass bowls and large stainless steel bowls! Glass is great for melting down butter or chocolate for a ganache in the microwave, and large stainless steel bowls are great for prep work and whisking your dry ingredients together. Check your local area for a restaurant supply store. You don't need any credentials to shop there, and you can find tools like piping tips, bowls, and other utensils at very low prices.

GLASS LIQUID MEASURING CUPS: I prefer to use heatproof glass measuring cups. I've poured hot brown butter into plastic cups before and had them warp, so stick to tempered glass measuring cups.

HEAT-RESISTANT SILICONE SPATULAS: Almost every recipe in this book requires you to stir ingredients together or scrape a pot or bowl. I like to use a silicone spatula so I can easily transition between working with hot or cold ingredients or mixtures. I also like to keep smaller spatulas on hand to be able to get into jars.

MEASURING SPOONS AND MEASURING CUPS: Invest in a good set of stainless steel measuring spoons and nested dry measuring cups (OXO makes my favorite tools). Plastic and wood measuring spoons can be cute, but are often not accurate!

ROLLING PINS: The two main rolling pins I use in my kitchen are a large untapered dowel type for recipes like cookie and yeasted doughs, and a smaller untapered dowel type for tortillas or buñuelos. These rolling pins give you better control and allow you to apply even pressure.

SCALE: To me, baking is like alchemy, so measurements need to be accurate if you want to be successful. Measuring cups can be inaccurate when it comes to lighter ingredients like flour and cocoa powder, so to make sure the recipe turns out the same every single time, use a scale to weigh out your ingredients.

STAND MIXER: I use a stand mixer to make all of my doughs, batters, whipped cream, and frostings.

THERMOMETERS: Get yourself some thermometers! I use three on a regular basis: an oven thermometer to make sure the temperature in my oven is accurate; an instant-read thermometer to check the internal temperature of bread loaves for doneness; and a clip-on candy thermometer to check the temperature of the oil for deep-frying (otherwise your buñuelos won't fry the way you want them to).

TORTILLA PRESS: A tortilla press is helpful for making the perfectly round tortilla, and we'll also be using it throughout the book to help us flatten the topping for our conchas, or flatten the topping for our rosca de reyes. Make sure to steer clear of aluminum tortilla presses, as they tend to break.

TORTILLA WARMER: This is a basket used to keep tortillas warm. In a pinch, placing the warm tortillas between two kitchen towels works just as well.

WHISKS: Whisks are going to be helpful when you're combining your wet and dry ingredients either separately or together. I typically switch between stainless steel whisks and rubber-coated whisks when I'm working with a nonstick pot or pan to make sure I don't scratch the surface.

Weights

The weight of 1 cup of flour can vary by baker, so I've compiled a table with the weights I used to develop the recipes in this book. OXO and All-Clad make my favorite measuring cups and spoons. Note that wooden cups and spoons and plastic sets often tend to be inaccurate!

INGREDIENT	1 CUP	½ CUP	⅓ CUP	¼ CUP
Butter, unsalted	227 g	115 g	76 g	57 g
Cocoa powder, Dutch process	90 g	45 g	30 g	22 g
Cornstarch	128 g	64 g	43 g	32 g
Dulce de leche	300 g	150 g	100 g	75 g
Flour, all-purpose	125 g	62 g	42 g	31 g
Guava paste	480 g	240 g	160 g	120 g
Lard	208 g	104 g	69 g	52 g
Masa harina (Maseca brand)	112 g	56 g	37 g	28 g
Mexican chocolate, grated	150 g	75 g	50 g	41 g
Shortening, vegetable	192 g	96 g	64 g	48 g
Sugar, granulated white	200 g	100 g	67 g	50 g
Sugar, light brown	208 g	104 g	69 g	52 g
Sugar, powdered	100 g	50 g	33 g	25 g
Sugar, turbinado	208 g	104 g	69 g	52 g

Tips

If you've never picked up a whisk before, I know that trying to bake anything from scratch can seem kind of confusing or intimidating. In my virtual cooking classes, I always like to suggest to new cooks or bakers to have a pen and paper handy when trying out a new recipe, as well as making sure to read through the recipe a couple of times and take notes. If the recipe calls for an ingredient or technique you've never heard of before, jot it down and look it up so you can be better prepared once you start cooking.

Another thing I like to suggest to new cooks or bakers is to practice mise en place, which simply means to measure and lay out all of your ingredients, so you can easily visualize what you are working with. This gives you an opportunity to check off the ingredients you've used as you cook or bake so you don't miss a thing.

The two most important tools you'll need for this book—and I can't repeat this enough—are a scale and an oven thermometer. When I bake, I like to weigh my ingredients. I found that when I wasn't using a scale to measure my flour, I was packing an extra ¼ cup of flour, which can greatly affect a recipe! Additionally, not all ovens are accurate, and using an oven thermometer will make sure that you are always baking at the correct temperature instead of under- and overcooking your desserts.

Cooking and baking in my culture has always been part of an oral tradition. We learn to cook by watching and listening to our elders, so I've created a visual guide on my website with a set of videos with step-by-step instructions for things like:

- How to brown butter
- How to shape telera rolls
- How to shape bolillo rolls
- How to fold orejitas
- How to fold tamales

And so much more! **Simply scan the QR code** for easy access.

You'll even get to peek into my pantry and learn about the ingredients I use and how to weigh out ingredients correctly. There's also an FAQ section on my website (chicanoeats.com/chicano-bakes-tips-techniques), where you can write to me and ask me questions—and I will answer you personally.

The smell of warm fresh tortillas always takes me back to being a kid and heading out to el jardín (the town square) to pick up a kilo of corn tortillas para mi abuelita Victoria. I would clutch a handful of pesos in my fist and would walk toward el jardín repeating "un kilo" in my head to make sure I didn't forget how much she needed. Making tortillas at home takes some practice, but once you get the hang of it, you can make the recipe your own by infusing your masa with chile puree, chopped herbs, or whatever else you feel like.

TORTILLAS DE MAÍZ
Corn Tortillas

Makes 12 tortillas

2 cups (224 g) Maseca masa
  harina

¾ teaspoon Diamond Crystal
  kosher salt or heaping
  ¼ teaspoon fine sea salt

1½ cups (354 g) hot water

✦ In a large bowl, whisk together the masa harina and salt, then pour in the water ¼ cup (59 g) at a time and use your hands to mix the dough until it comes together into a smooth ball. Once the dough has come together, place it in a bowl and cover with plastic wrap. Let the dough sit for 20 minutes to allow it to fully hydrate.

✦ After the dough has sat for 20 minutes, place a comal (flat round skillet), large nonstick skillet, or cast-iron skillet over high heat. I like to let the comal, nonstick skillet, or cast-iron skillet sit over the heat for 4 to 5 minutes to make sure it is extremely hot. While you wait, divide the dough into 12 balls (about 47 g each), then prep your tortilla press. Grab a 1-gallon resealable plastic bag and cut it at the seams so you have two equal squares. Open the tortilla press and place one of the plastic squares on the bottom plate of the press, place a ball of dough on top of it, then cover with the second plastic square. Close the press and press down to flatten the dough into a 5½-inch (14 cm) tortilla.

✦ Gently peel off the top piece of plastic, flip the tortilla over onto your palm, and gently peel off the back piece of plastic. Place the tortilla onto the hot skillet and cook for 30 seconds, then flip the tortilla and let cook for another 30 seconds. Flip the tortilla again and cook for 10 seconds, then use your hand or a spatula to press the center of the tortilla; this will make the tortilla puff up.

✦ Flip the tortilla one more time and let cook for an additional 10 seconds, then use a spatula to remove it from the skillet. Wrap it in a kitchen towel so the residual steam finishes cooking it as you finish the rest.

NOTE: I developed this tortilla recipe using Maseca corn flour because it is more accessible, but if you are able to splurge on good-quality corn flour, check out Masienda, which makes my favorite blue and white corn flour from single-origin heirloom corn from Mexico. This flour makes for really great sopes, tortillas, and chochoyotes! Masienda's corn flour, along with Bob's Red Mill's, will require more hydration than Maseca.

I love flour tortillas, and I like making them from scratch, especially when I have leftover bacon grease. Substitute bacon grease, melted butter, or ghee for the lard for even more flavor. You can also use vegetable shortening instead of lard for vegan-friendly flour tortillas! Making perfectly round tortillas is a skill that comes with time and practice, so don't be afraid to embrace organic shapes as you learn. I've developed this recipe to make small (6-inch) tortillas so they can easily fit on smaller skillets, but I'm also including instructions below for those who might want to make larger tortillas.

TORTILLAS DE HARINA
Flour Tortillas

Makes twelve 6-inch (15 cm) tortillas

2½ cups (312 g) unbleached all-purpose flour

1½ teaspoons Diamond Crystal kosher salt or ¾ teaspoon fine sea salt

1 teaspoon baking powder

¾ cup (177 g) hot water

⅓ cup (69 g) lard, melted

+ In the bowl of a stand mixer, whisk together the flour, kosher salt, and baking powder. Fit the stand mixer with the dough hook, then turn the speed on to low. Slowly pour in the hot water. Once fully incorporated, pour in the melted lard. Gradually bump the speed up to medium-high and let the dough knead for 5 minutes, until it comes together into a smooth ball.

+ Cover the bowl with plastic wrap and let sit for 20 minutes to let the dough fully hydrate.

+ Divide the dough into 12 balls (about 45 g each), then use a rolling pin to roll the balls into thin 6-inch (15 cm) rounds. The best way to get a perfect circle is to roll the dough, then turn it, roll, then turn, to make sure the pressure is being distributed equally.

+ Place a comal or a large dry skillet over medium heat and let it sit for 4 to 5 minutes to make sure it's hot. Cook each tortilla for 20 seconds on each side. Place them in a tortilla warmer to steam while you finish cooking the rest.

NOTE: For larger flour tortillas, double the recipe and divide the dough into 12 balls (about 90 g each). Roll each ball into a 12-inch (30 cm) round. Place a large skillet over medium heat and cook the tortilla for 30 seconds on one side, flip, and then cook for another 30 seconds. Flip again and cook for 15 seconds, and then flip once more and cook for 15 more seconds.

Telera rolls are soft and pillowy rolls of bread usually used to make tortas (sandwiches) in Mexico. I like to add lard to my rolls to keep them soft and moist, but you can easily make them vegan or vegetarian-friendly by using vegetable shortening instead. Make sure to keep the teleras stored in a resealable plastic bag overnight, otherwise they will dry out and turn rock hard!

TELERAS
Telera Rolls

Makes 6 rolls

½ cup (118 g) slightly hot water (100° to 110°F/38° to 43°C)

1 tablespoon sugar

1 tablespoon active dry yeast

6¼ cups (781 g) unbleached all-purpose flour, plus more for dusting

1 tablespoon Diamond Crystal kosher salt or 1½ teaspoons fine sea salt

1½ cups (354 g) warm water

3 tablespoons lard or vegetable shortening

✦ In a measuring cup with the slightly hot water (not warm but not scalding hot either, which will kill the yeast), stir together the sugar and yeast. Let this mixture sit for about 10 minutes until it is nice and bubbly. If your yeast doesn't start bubbling, the water might have been too hot and killed it, so you'll have to start over.

✦ In the bowl of a stand mixer, whisk together the flour and salt, then attach the dough hook.

✦ Turn the speed to low, then slowly pour in the yeast mixture and knead for 1 minute. Pour in the 1½ cups (354 g) warm water, then, once all of the water has been incorporated, add the lard or shortening. Turn the speed up to medium-low and let the dough knead until it comes together into a ball, about 2 minutes. Once the dough has come together, turn the speed up to medium, and let it knead for 4 minutes.

✦ Lightly grease a large bowl with a quick spritz of cooking spray and turn the dough out into the bowl. Cover the bowl with plastic wrap and set in a warm place to hang out until doubled in size, about 1½ hours.

✦ Once the dough has risen, punch it down and turn it out onto a floured surface. Let the dough rest for 5 minutes, then divide it into 6 equal-size balls (about 208 g each).

✦ Line two baking sheets with parchment paper.

✦ Lightly dust the surface with more flour, then take one of the dough balls and add a light dusting of flour to the top. Use the palm of your hand to gently flatten the ball, then stretch it slightly to form an oval. Use your fingers to further stretch the dough into an oval 6 to 7 inches (15 to 18 cm) long and 2 to 3 inches (5 to 7.5 cm) wide. Place the oval on the lined baking sheet. Repeat this process with the rest of the dough, placing 3 rolls per baking sheet so they have enough room to bake. Sprinkle each oval with

(continues)

flour, then use a chopstick or metal straw to press two lengthwise parallel indentations into the dough, dividing the top of the roll roughly into thirds. Make sure you only add enough pressure to score the dough and make the indentations but not cut through the dough.

✦ Lightly spritz a large piece of plastic wrap with nonstick spray, then loosely drape each baking sheet with a piece of plastic wrap and let the teleras proof in a dark and warm place until doubled in size, about 1 hour.

✦ Preheat the oven to 350°F (180°C).

✦ Gently remove the plastic wrap, then bake the teleras until the tops are golden, 33 to 36 minutes. Let them cool for 10 to 15 minutes before eating.

Bolillos are rolls related to the French baguette. They are little loaves of bread that have a crunchy outer shell with a pillowy inside and are often used for tortas (sandwiches). The trick to getting that crunchy outer shell is to place a water bath at the bottom of the oven to make sure the environment is nice and steamy for the loaves as they bake. I love slicing a warm bolillo in half and filling it with refried beans and queso fresco for a simple breakfast or a torta for on the go.

BOLILLOS
Bolillo Rolls

Makes 6 rolls

1⅔ cups (393 g) slightly hot water (100° to 110°F/38° to 43°C)

1 tablespoon active dry yeast

1 tablespoon sugar

5¼ cups (656 g) unbleached all-purpose flour, plus more for dusting

1 tablespoon Diamond Crystal kosher salt or 1½ teaspoons fine sea salt

2 tablespoons lard or vegetable shortening

¼ cup (56 g) neutral oil, such as avocado or vegetable

✦ In a measuring cup filled with 1 cup (236 g) of the slightly hot water, mix together the yeast and sugar. Let sit for 10 minutes to activate.

✦ In a stand mixer fitted with the dough hook, whisk together the flour and salt. Set the stand mixer on low speed and slowly pour in the yeast mixture. Pour in the remaining ⅔ cup (157 g) slightly hot water, then add the lard. Increase the speed to medium-low and let the dough come together; it should take 2 to 3 minutes.

✦ Once the dough has come together, turn up the speed to medium and let the dough knead for an additional 4 minutes. Spritz a large bowl with cooking spray, transfer the dough to the bowl, cover with plastic wrap, and let sit in a dark warm place to proof until doubled in size, about 2 hours.

✦ Line two baking sheets with parchment paper, then set aside.

✦ After the dough has doubled in size, divide it into 6 equal portions (about 178 g each). Lightly dust a work surface with flour, then grab a ball of dough and use the palm of your hand to flatten it into an oval 5 to 6 inches (12.5 to 15 cm) long and 2 to 3 inches (5 to 7.5 cm) wide. (I like to flatten the dough, stretch it, then wait a minute and repeat this process until I have an oval long enough to work with.)

✦ Once you have the ovals rolled out, take the top edge of one and roll it toward you, then use your fingers to pinch and seal it, rolling and pinching seams together until you have a roll. Evenly space 3 rolls per baking sheet, then lightly brush each roll with the neutral oil. Lightly spritz a large piece of plastic wrap with nonstick spray then loosely drape each baking sheet with plastic wrap and place in a warm spot until the dough has doubled in size, about 1 hour.

(continues)

✦ About 30 minutes before the rolls are done proofing, fill a large roasting dish with 8 cups (2 liters) warm water and place the water bath on the very bottom of the oven. Preheat the oven to 425°F (220°C). The water bath needs to be in there at least 30 minutes before the rolls go in to ensure the oven is steamy. The steam is what gives the bolillos a crunchy outer shell.

✦ Once the rolls are doubled in size, use a thin sharp knife or razor to score a 4-inch (10 cm) line into the center of each roll. Bake one baking sheet at a time until the tops are nice and golden brown, 32 to 36 minutes. Replenish the water bath as needed. Let the rolls rest for 10 to 15 minutes before serving.

If you're vegan or lactose-intolerant, this dairy-free caramel sauce is for you! It's made with coconut milk and sugar, which, once reduced, turns into this rich, toasty, and luscious caramel sauce (reminiscent of caramel corn) that you can pour over pancakes, ice cream, or gorditas de azúcar.

DAIRY-FREE COCONUT CARAMEL SAUCE

Makes about 2 cups (475 ml)

2 (13.5oz/400 g) cans full-fat
coconut milk

1 cup (200 g) granulated white
sugar

¾ cup (155 g) light brown sugar

1 teaspoon pure vanilla extract

¼ teaspoon baking soda

¼ teaspoon Diamond Crystal
kosher salt or ⅛ teaspoon
fine sea salt

✦ In a stockpot, place the coconut milk over medium heat. Once all the fat has melted, whisk in both sugars, the vanilla, baking soda, and salt and let the mixture come to a boil, about 10 to 12 minutes.

✦ When the mixture has reached a boil, reduce the heat to medium-low and simmer until the caramel is dark brown and easily coats the back of a spoon, 37 to 42 minutes, stirring only occasionally (overstirring will cause it to crystallize).

✦ Let cool completely, then pour into a jar, straining out any leftover little bits of brown sugar to ensure that the sauce is totally smooth. Let it sit in the refrigerator overnight so the flavors develop further. This caramel should be stored in an airtight jar or container in the refrigerator; it will keep for 3 to 4 weeks if stored properly.

Homemade whipped cream is top tier. You can easily customize it with the addition of rum, vanilla bean paste, and liqueurs, which makes it so much better than store-bought. I like to use a few tablespoons of hazelnut liqueur for added flavor, and I also like to add sour cream, as that gives it a nice tang and helps stabilize the whipped cream so you can use it as a whipped topping for my Tres Leches cake (page 136)!

CREMA BATIDA
Whipped Cream

Makes about 3 cups (315 g)

1 cup (227 g) heavy whipping
cream

¼ cup (60 g) sour cream

2 tablespoons hazelnut liqueur
(optional)

1½ teaspoons vanilla bean paste
or pure vanilla extract

¼ cup (25 g) powdered sugar

✦ In the bowl of a stand mixer, combine the heavy cream, sour cream, hazelnut liqueur (if using), and vanilla bean paste. Sift in the powdered sugar, then fit the stand mixer with the whisk. Gradually bump the speed up from low to medium, then whip the heavy cream for 1 minute 45 seconds for soft peaks, 2½ minutes for medium peaks, and 3 to 3 minutes 15 seconds for firm peaks.

Cajeta is a rich caramel sauce similar to dulce de leche but made with goat's milk. You can make it the classic way with goat's milk (the directions are the same), but I prefer to use cow's milk because I like the flavor better. I also take my cajeta a step further by adding rum or bourbon, brown sugar, and cinnamon to give the sauce even more dimension. You can drizzle cajeta over pancakes, ice cream, waffles, gorditas de azucar, or on a warm bolillo. Make sure to use a tall stainless steel stockpot to make cajeta; if you use a short stockpot, the cajeta might foam over as the moisture starts to evaporate.

CAJETA ENVINADA
Cinnamon Rum Cajeta Sauce

Makes about 2 cups (475 ml)

4 cups (944 g) whole milk
or goat's milk
¼ cup (60 g) rum or bourbon
1 cup (200 g) granulated sugar
¼ cup (52 g) light brown sugar
½ teaspoon baking soda
1 large Mexican cinnamon stick

✦ In a large stockpot, whisk together the milk, rum, granulated sugar, brown sugar, and baking soda. Add in the cinnamon stick. Place the pot over medium heat and bring to a boil; it should take 12 to 15 minutes. Once it reaches a boil, reduce the heat to medium-low and set a timer for 45 minutes. At this point, you'll need to babysit the sauce for the next 10 minutes and whisk often to prevent it from foaming over as the moisture evaporates.

✦ Keep an eye on the timer and let the cajeta simmer over medium-low for a total of 40 to 45 minutes, until it starts to thicken, stirring occasionally. Keep in mind that it will thicken even more as it cools, so don't cook it past 45 minutes, or you'll end up with hard candy.

✦ Remove the cinnamon stick and let the cajeta cool completely before straining into a jar and letting it sit in the refrigerator overnight so the flavors develop further. Cajeta should be stored in an airtight jar or container in the refrigerator and will keep for 3 to 4 weeks if stored properly.

Making vanilla extract is a fairly easy task—the hardest part is having to wait 6 weeks to be able to use it—and the end product is worth it. Vodka is perfect for this because the clean flavor lets the vanilla bean shine, but you can also use bourbon to give the extract even more depth and dimension and add notes of caramel. (Sometimes I like to use a mix of both spirits and use 9 ounces of vodka and 3 ounces of bourbon.) Whenever I make my own extract, I like to make a few extra batches as gifts to friends and family for Christmas!

VANILLA EXTRACT

Makes 1½ cups (355 ml)

6 vanilla beans
Pinch of salt
**1½ cups (355 g) vodka
or bourbon**

✦ Wash well and dry thoroughly a 12-ounce (355 ml) mason jar or container with a lid. Use a paring knife to split the vanilla beans lengthwise down the middle, then use the back of the knife blade to scrape out the seeds and transfer them to the container. Fold the vanilla bean pods in half to make sure they fit and add them to the container and sprinkle in the salt.

✦ Pour the vodka into a small saucepan and bring it to a slight simmer over medium-low heat. Once small bubbles start to form around the rim of the saucepan and the liquid starts to come to a simmer, remove the saucepan from the heat. Carefully funnel the vodka into the container, then let it cool completely. Once cooled, place the lid on and use a piece of tape to label the extract with the date and store in a dark cupboard for at least 6 weeks.

Dulce de leche is similar to cajeta, and is typically made using cow's milk and granulated sugar. There are a few different ways to make dulce de leche (and I tested them all!), but I found that making it on the stovetop yields the best results because it gives you better control. Making dulce de leche in the oven took too long, and the consistency wasn't great. Using a pressure cooker to make it can be dangerous, and boiling a can of condensed milk just makes it hard to know when it's done since you can't see inside the can.

DULCE DE LECHE

Makes about 2 cups (475 ml)

4 cups (944 g) whole milk

1¼ cups (250 g) sugar

1 teaspoon vanilla extract

¼ teaspoon baking soda

¼ teaspoon Diamond Crystal kosher salt or ⅛ teaspoon fine sea salt

➤ In a large stockpot, whisk together the milk, sugar, vanilla, baking soda, and salt and bring to a boil over medium heat, which should take 12 to 15 minutes. Once the mixture reaches a boil, reduce the heat to medium-low and set a timer for 45 minutes. At this point, you'll need to babysit the sauce for the next 10 minutes and whisk often to prevent it from foaming over as moisture evaporates.

➤ Let the dulce de leche simmer over medium-low for a total of 40 to 45 minutes, stirring occasionally. Keep in mind that the sauce will thicken as it cools, so don't cook it past 45 minutes, or you'll end up with hard candy.

➤ Let the dulce de leche cool completely, then strain and transfer to a jar and refrigerate overnight for the flavors to develop further. Dulce de leche should be stored in an airtight jar or container in the refrigerator, and will keep for 3 to 4 weeks if stored properly.

PAN DULCE MEXICANO

Welcome to the pan dulce chapter! For me, this was the hardest chapter to work on because there are just so many different types of pan dulce to choose from. According to CANAINPA (la Cámara Nacional de la Industria Panificadora), over 750 types of pan dulce have been registered in Mexico. I ended up sticking with my personal favorites, and chose the ones that you are more likely to run into at a panadería in the US. I tried to keep most recipes as traditional as possible, but you're going to find some where I've adjusted things, like in the recipe for marranitos. These are gingerbread pigs that are typically very dry and crumbly and usually need to be eaten with a drink like a warm cup of café con leche, but I make them moist and cakey, so I can actually enjoy them on their own! I know you're going to run into certain recipes where you might ask, can I use butter instead of vegetable shortening? And the answer is, of course! Just note that in many cases (like with any of the polvorones), using butter instead of shortening will change the texture of the recipe, since shortening is all fat, and butter contains extra moisture.

MEXICAN SWEET BREAD

Conchas are fluffy little buns that have a shell (concha) design scored onto their sugary streusel topping, which is what gives them their name. (They've become an icon for pan dulce in the United States.) Conchas come in all sorts of colors, like pink, white, and orange, and in many different flavors, like chocolate or matcha—and they are so good accompanied with a hot cup of Chocolate Caliente (page 200).

CONCHAS
Vanilla Conchas

Makes 12 buns

FOR THE CONCHAS

½ cup (118 g) whole milk

½ cup (100 g) plus 1 tablespoon sugar

1 tablespoon active dry yeast

4 cups (500 g) unbleached all-purpose flour

1 teaspoon Diamond Crystal kosher salt or ½ teaspoon fine sea salt

½ cup (8 tablespoons/115 g) unsalted butter, melted

2 large eggs

FOR THE TOPPING

1 cup (125 g) all-purpose flour

1¼ cups (125 g) powdered sugar, sifted

½ teaspoon baking powder

¼ teaspoon kosher salt or pinch of fine sea salt

½ cup (96 g) butter-flavored vegetable shortening

1½ teaspoons vanilla extract

Gel food coloring (optional; see Tip on page 46)

FOR THE EGG WASH

1 large egg, whisked

✦ **Make the conchas:** In a measuring cup or heatproof bowl, whisk together the milk, ¼ cup (59 g) water, and 1 tablespoon of the sugar. Pop it in the microwave for 35 to 45 seconds until this mixture is just slightly hot to the touch. (If it's burning hot, it'll kill the yeast.) For better accuracy, use a thermometer and heat this mixture to 110° to 115°F/43° to 46°C. Stir in the yeast, then let the mixture bloom for 10 minutes, until nice and bubbly. (If it doesn't bloom, the milk mixture was too hot and killed the yeast; you'll need to start over.)

✦ In the bowl of a stand mixer, whisk together the flour, remaining ½ cup (100 g) sugar, and salt. Snap on the dough hook. Turn the mixer speed to low and pour in the yeast mixture. Once it's been incorporated, beat in the melted butter, then beat in the eggs, one at a time. Increase the speed to medium-low and let the dough come together for 2 minutes. Turn the mixer off, use a rubber spatula to scrape down the sides, and let the dough mix on medium-high for a final 4 minutes. The dough will be sticky, so make sure you're using a sturdy rubber spatula.

✦ Lightly mist a large bowl with cooking spray. Use a spatula to scrape the dough into the oiled bowl, then cover with plastic wrap. Place the dough in a warm and dark place and let proof until doubled in size, 2 to 2½ hours.

✦ Remove the plastic wrap, lightly grease your hands, and punch the dough down. Let it sit for 5 minutes while you make the topping.

✦ **Make the topping:** In a medium bowl, whisk together the flour, powdered sugar, baking powder, and salt and set aside. In a clean stand mixer bowl, add the shortening. Fit the mixer with the paddle and beat on low speed for 1 minute, then add half of the flour mixture. Once the flour has been incorporated, add the vanilla extract, followed by the remaining flour mixture. Scrape down the sides of the bowl, then beat until the topping comes together, 2 to 3 minutes; it should feel like soft Play-Doh. If you'd like to add some color to your topping, do so now (see Tip on page 46).

(continues)

✦ Divide the topping into balls of dough that weigh 25 grams each. This should give you 12 balls of dough, and an extra portion for cushion. Cover with plastic wrap to prevent them from drying out.

✦ With clean hands, divide the concha dough into 12 equal portions (about 84 g each) and roll into smooth balls. The dough will feel a little sticky but not wet. Grease your hands to prevent any dough from sticking; however, do not add any extra flour to your dough.

✦ Line three 13 × 18-inch (33 × 45 cm) baking sheets with parchment paper. Evenly space 4 balls of dough per lined pan, then lightly brush each ball of dough with some egg wash.

✦ Take a ball of topping and place it in between two sheets of plastic (I like to cut a 1-gallon resealable plastic bag in two), then use a tortilla press, or a small plate, to gently flatten the ball into a disc 3.5 inches (9 cm) wide (the topping will expand as it bakes, so do not make it too thin). Peel the disc off the plastic and into your hand, then place it on top of a ball of dough and gently press it into the dough to lightly flatten the ball. Use a sharp knife or stencil to score a shell design onto the topping. Repeat for the remaining portions of topping.

✦ Lightly spritz a large piece of plastic wrap with nonstick spray, then loosely drape the conchas with plastic wrap and let rise in a warm and dark place for 1 hour. (Make sure to not pull the plastic wrap over the baking sheet because that will pin the conchas down, and they need to rise vertically.)

✦ About 30 minutes before the conchas have finished rising, preheat the oven to 350°F (180°C).

✦ Gently peel off the plastic wrap, then bake the conchas, one tray at a time, until the topping has risen and they look golden brown, 16 to 18 minutes. Let cool on a wire rack for 6 to 8 minutes before serving. Store any leftover conchas in a resealable plastic bag or airtight container to prevent them from drying out.

TIP: To incorporate color into the conchas, divide the topping into as many colors as you'd like and knead a few drops of gel food coloring into each ball of topping. Do not use liquid food coloring, as it will add extra moisture to the topping and make it sticky to work with. Gel food coloring can be purchased at your local cake supply store, local craft store, and online!

The roles de canela you find at the panadería typically have a thin layer of icing and will often surprise you with a raisin or two in them. But don't worry, there's no raisins in mine. While cinnamon rolls are already perfect, cinnamon rolls with dulce de leche cream cheese icing are even better. For this recipe, you can let the dough rise and bake in a few hours, but I recommend letting the dough proof overnight; it makes the dough easier to work with and results in a prettier and more swirly cinnamon roll. I'm including two icing recipes: a classic vanilla bean cream cheese icing and a fluffy dulce de leche frosting. Because porque no los dos?

ROLES DE CANELA
Cinnamon Rolls

Makes 12 rolls

FOR THE DOUGH

¼ cup (59 g) slightly hot water (100° to 110°F/38° to 43°C)

1 (7 g) envelope active dry yeast (2¼ teaspoons)

½ cup (8 tablespoons/115 g) unsalted butter

¾ cup (172 g) buttermilk

2 large eggs, at room temperature

¼ cup (50 g) granulated sugar

½ teaspoon Diamond Crystal kosher salt or ¼ teaspoon fine sea salt

3¾ cups (469 g) unbleached all-purpose flour

(continues)

✦ **Make the dough:** Place the hot water in a small bowl, sprinkle the yeast over, and carefully mix it in. Set aside to bloom.

✦ In a small saucepan, melt the butter over medium-low heat, making sure it doesn't start to bubble up at all. Once the butter has melted, remove the pan from the heat and stir in the buttermilk. This helps cool down the butter while warming up the buttermilk at the same time; making sure the butter isn't too hot here is important so the buttermilk doesn't break/curdle.

✦ Set this mixture aside and check to make sure the yeast has bloomed properly; the yeast should be bubbly. If it hasn't bubbled up after 10 minutes, the water temperature could be off or the yeast might be dead. Try again! You can use a quick-read thermometer to make sure the water's temperature is 100° to 110°F/38° to 43°C; you can also add a pinch of sugar to help the yeast activate more quickly.

✦ In the bowl of a stand mixer, combine the eggs, granulated sugar, and salt and stir with a silicone spatula to combine. Stir in the butter-buttermilk mixture and give that another stir. Add about half the flour and stir by hand, then add the rest of the flour with the yeast mixture and place the bowl onto the stand mixer fitted with the dough hook. Turn the mixer on medium speed and wait until the dough hook has mixed everything together, then let the machine knead the dough until it has mostly pulled away from the sides of the bowl but is still sticking to the bottom, 5 to 7 minutes. The dough should be slightly sticky, but this means it's got a nice hydration and will be a beautiful perfect soft fluffy cinnamon roll in the end.

(continues)

FOR THE FILLING

¼ cup (4 tablespoons/57 g) unsalted butter, melted

¾ cup (156 g) light brown sugar

1 tablespoon ground cinnamon

Pinch of salt

FOR THE TOPPING
(CHOOSE ONE OR BOTH)

Fluffy Dulce de Leche Frosting (recipe follows)

Classic Vanilla Bean Cream Cheese Icing (recipe follows)

✦ Mist a large bowl with nonstick cooking spray, then transfer the dough to the bowl, using a silicone spatula to scrape out any stickier dough that might still be in the mixer bowl. Sort of form the dough into a ball, flipping it over so the top is smooth and has the oil from the spray on it. Cover with plastic wrap.

For the first proofing of the dough there are two options:

✦ **Same day:** If you want the cinnamon rolls to be finished in a few hours, set the dough aside to proof at room temperature in a draft-free space until it has doubled in size, 1½ to 2 hours.

✦ **Overnight:** To bake the next day, proof the dough in the refrigerator overnight (at least 7 hours and up to 24). This is my preferred method because it allows the dough to be a little more hands off and makes it so it's less work to finish the rolls in the morning. It also allows the butter to firm up, making the rolling out and up of the dough much easier, giving you less hassle and a prettier swirl on the finished roll.

After dough is done proofing:

✦ **Make the filling:** Once the dough has proofed, prepare the filling by mixing together the melted butter, brown sugar, cinnamon, and salt to form a paste. Set aside.

✦ Roll out the dough on a generously floured counter into a rectangle (see Tip on page 50) 13 × 18 inches (33 × 46 cm) with the short dimension facing you. Carefully spread the filling over the dough, leaving about ½ inch (1.25 cm) or so on the two longer sides without filling (we're going to trim off the ends, so no need to waste filling). Starting on a short side, carefully roll up the dough from one shorter end to another; I like to start at the top of the rectangle and roll it up tightly toward me.

✦ Grease a 9 × 13-inch (23 × 33 cm) baking pan and set aside. Trim the ends off the dough log to make sure the cinnamon rolls will be flat on both sides, then carefully slice the log into 12 even rolls. I like to use a serrated bread knife and carefully make tiny cuts to mark the rolls, first marking the dough with 3 cuts to get 4 even sections, then marking each section in the log into thirds to get 12 even rolls. No need for a ruler this early in the morning. Use just the weight of the bread knife to slowly and carefully slice each roll to get the cleanest cuts. As you cut the rolls, carefully transfer

(continues)

them to the baking pan in 4 rows of 3. Once all the rolls have been placed in the pan, place a piece of plastic wrap over the top and let the rolls rise until they are about doubled in size, about 1 hour. If you had an overnight proof, the dough might still be a little cold and need about 15 extra minutes to proof.

✦ About 30 minutes before the dough has proofed, preheat the oven to 350°F (180°C).

✦ Remove the plastic wrap and bake the rolls just until they turn golden brown, 20 to 25 minutes, making sure you don't overbake and dry them out.

✦ **Meanwhile, make the icing:** Follow the instructions opposite for Fluffy Dulce de Leche Frosting or Classic Vanilla Bean Cream Cheese Icing. Remove the rolls from the oven and let them sit for 10 minutes before icing them with your desired topping.

✦ Serve the rolls warm for maximum softness. If someone shows up late and they've cooled, just reheat them in the microwave for 15 to 20 seconds to soften them back up. Store any leftover rolls in the refrigerator for up to 1 day; any longer than that and they tend to be too tough and dried out. Cinnamon roll perfection exists the same day they're baked, but even a day-old microwaved cinnamon roll fixes a lot of problems.

TIP: The measurement for the rectangle of dough is actually the size of a half-sheet pan, so to make my life easier I flip a half-sheet pan over onto the work surface before flouring and use a small piece of masking tape to mark off each corner to give me a rough idea how big the rectangle needs to be. That way there's no need for a ruler or tape measure first thing in the morning before you've had any coffee.

FLUFFY DULCE DE LECHE FROSTING

Makes enough for 12 rolls

4 ounces (115 g) full-fat cream cheese, at room temperature

¼ cup (4 tablespoons/57 g) unsalted butter, at room temperature

½ cup (150 g) dulce de leche (see page 41)

½ cup (50 g) powdered sugar, sifted

2 tablespoons heavy cream

Pinch of salt

✦ In a stand mixer fitted with the paddle, combine all the ingredients and mix on low speed just to combine. Increase the speed to medium-high and paddle until the frosting is well mixed.

CLASSIC VANILLA BEAN CREAM CHEESE ICING

Makes enough for 12 rolls

4 ounces (115 g) full-fat cream cheese, at room temperature

¼ cup (4 tablespoons/57 g) unsalted butter, at room temperature

1 cup (100 g) powdered sugar, sifted

1 teaspoon vanilla bean paste or pure vanilla extract

1 tablespoon heavy cream or milk

Pinch of salt

✦ In a stand mixer fitted with the paddle, combine all the ingredients and mix on low speed just to combine. Increase the speed to medium-high and paddle until the icing is well mixed.

Mantecadas are sweet muffins typically wrapped in a red liner that you are likely to stumble on at your local panadería, as mantecadas are a staple when it comes to pan dulce. I tested these more times than I can count, and although the name implies that they're made with manteca (lard), I found that using a neutral oil produced a lighter crumb. The fluffy dome is another indicator of a perfect mantecada, and the trick to achieving it? That's a secret I'll never tell. xoxo. Just kidding: It's a slight rest and an extra-hot oven. Follow the instructions closely and you'll get a perfect mantecada every time.

MANTECADAS
Sweet Muffins

Makes 18 muffins

2 cups (250 g) unbleached
    all-purpose flour

2 teaspoons baking powder

½ teaspoon baking soda

1 teaspoon Diamond Crystal
    kosher salt or ½ teaspoon
    fine sea salt

1¼ cups (250 g) sugar

1 cup (236 g) whole milk

½ cup (112 g) neutral oil,
    such as canola or avocado

2 large eggs

1 tablespoon pure vanilla extract

✦ Line 12 cups of a standard muffin tin with paper liners. Line 6 cups of a second tin with paper liners. (See Note.) Set aside.

✦ In a large bowl, whisk together the flour, baking powder, baking soda, and salt. In another bowl, whisk together the sugar, milk, oil, eggs, and vanilla. Add the wet ingredients to the dry ingredients and whisk together just until combined and no traces of flour remain.

✦ Fill each lined muffin cup with about 3 tablespoons of batter and set aside uncovered for 30 minutes.

✦ While the batter rests, preheat the oven to 425°F (220°C). The combo of the resting and high heat will help give the muffins that nice perfect top.

✦ Slide the muffins into the oven to bake for 7 minutes. Reduce the oven temperature to 400°F (200°C) and bake until they have puffed up, are slightly golden brown, and a toothpick inserted into the center of one comes out clean, 7 to 8 minutes longer.

✦ Let the muffins cool in the pans for 15 minutes, then carefully remove them and place them on a wire rack to cool completely.

✦ Store the muffins at room temperature sealed or lightly wrapped with plastic wrap. They will keep up to 3 days.

NOTE: If you've only got one tin to work with, just bake the first 12 muffins and bake the rest once the first batch has baked and the tin has cooled; the batter can sit in the bowl for a little bit longer and rest while you wait.

Marranitos are pig-shaped molasses and gingerbread cookies, and this is the pan dulce recipe that I am well known for! Traditionally these are dry and crumbly, but my version incorporates buttermilk to make sure these cookies stay nice and soft and moist. With reviews like "You really nailed this recipe! These are my dad's favorite cookie. Easy to make and they turn out perfect every time. Thank you!" I just know you're going to love them! Per tradition, this recipe calls for a pig-shaped cookie cutter, but any cookie cutter shape works!

MARRANITOS
Mexican Gingerbread Pig Cookies

Makes about 15 large cookies

FOR THE COOKIES

4½ cups (562 g) unbleached all-purpose flour, plus more for rolling out

1½ teaspoons ground cinnamon

1 teaspoon ground ginger

½ teaspoon ground allspice

1½ teaspoons baking powder

1 teaspoon baking soda

1 teaspoon Diamond Crystal kosher salt or ½ teaspoon fine sea salt

10 tablespoons (143 g) unsalted butter, at room temperature

1⅓ cups (277 g) dark brown sugar

¼ cup (84 g) molasses

¼ cup (57 g) buttermilk, at room temperature

2 large eggs, at room temperature

FOR THE EGG WASH

1 large egg whisked with 1 tablespoon cold water

✦ In a large bowl, whisk together the flour, cinnamon, ginger, allspice, baking powder, baking soda, and salt. Set aside.

✦ In a stand mixer fitted with the paddle, cream the butter and brown sugar on medium speed for 2 minutes, until fluffy. Reduce the speed to low, then slowly pour in the molasses and buttermilk. Add the eggs, one at a time, making sure that each egg is mixed in before adding the next. Add the flour mixture in three additions, incorporating well after each before adding the next. Scrape down the sides of the bowl, then beat for a final 30 seconds on medium-low speed.

✦ Divide the dough into 3 equal portions, form into balls, wrap in plastic wrap, and refrigerate for 4 hours, so the dough chills and is easier to work with.

✦ Preheat the oven to 350°F (180°C) and line three 13 × 18-inch (33 × 45 cm) baking sheets with parchment paper. On a well-floured surface, roll out one of the balls of dough to about a ⅓-inch (8 mm) thickness. Use a large pig-shaped cookie cutter to cut out the cookies (you should be able to get about 5 large cookies per ball of dough), then evenly space them on a lined baking sheet. I like to dip my cookie cutter in a little bit of flour to make sure I get clean edges. Repeat this process with the remaining balls of cookie dough.

✦ Once you have the cookies on the baking sheet, brush on the egg wash. Bake until the cookies have risen and the tops have begun to crack, 10 to 12 minutes.

✦ Let the cookies cool on the baking sheet for about 10 minutes before serving. Serve warm.

To make the ultimate Mexican wedding cookie, I decided to stick with toasted pecans and upgraded the nuttiness by incorporating brown butter and hazelnut liqueur for three layers of flavor. Feel free to use any nut in these cookies: pecans, pistachios, walnuts, cashews, almonds, and more all work. If the nuts are already toasted or roasted when you purchase them, skip the toasting step in the recipe.

BESITOS DE NUEZ
Mexican Wedding Cookies

Makes 30 cookies

1 cup (16 tablespoons/227 g)
  unsalted butter

1 cup (106 g) pecans

1½ cups (150 g) powdered sugar

1 tablespoon hazelnut liqueur
  or milk

1 teaspoon pure vanilla extract

½ teaspoon Diamond Crystal
  kosher salt or fine sea salt

1⅔ cups (208 g) unbleached
  all-purpose flour

✦ In a medium stainless steel saucepan or skillet, melt the butter over medium heat and wait for it to start fizzling and foaming, stirring occasionally with a silicone spatula to make sure nothing burns or sticks to the bottom of the pan. As the butter fizzles, the milk solids toast/brown, giving the finished product a hint of toffee flavor. Once the fizzling stops it's time to start checking for doneness. You want the melted liquid to be a golden color and there to be golden brown toasted milk solids on the bottom of the pan. From start to finish this should take about 12 minutes. Place the brown butter in a heatproof measuring cup, making sure to scrape all the flavorful browned bits off the bottom of the pan along with it. You should be left with just over ¾ cup (175 g) of liquid browned butter. Set this in the refrigerator for about 1 hour or so to firm up to about the consistency of room temperature butter.

✦ Preheat the oven to 350°F (180°C).

✦ Place the pecans on a small baking sheet and toast them in the oven for 7 to 8 minutes, carefully shaking the pan at about the 4-minute mark to make sure they don't burn. Once they're toasted, tip them out onto a large plate to cool for a few minutes, then finely chop them in a food processor or with a knife and set aside. Leave the oven on.

✦ In a stand mixer fitted with the paddle, beat the brown butter, ½ cup (50 g) of the powdered sugar, the hazelnut liqueur, vanilla, and salt together for a full 2 minutes. The full time is important because all that air whipped into the cookies helps give you the melt-in-your-mouth texture. You should see the mixture go from a tan color to an almost white color and it will have grown in volume, too.

✦ With the mixer on low, add the flour and pecans and mix until the dough comes together. It will look dry and crumbly at first but after mixing for about 30 seconds it should form a cohesive dough.

(continues)

✦ Line one 13 × 18-inch (33 × 45 cm) baking sheet with parchment paper, then roll out tablespoon-size balls of dough and place all 30 on the baking sheet. These don't spread very much, so you can place them about 1 inch (2.5 cm) apart to bake.

✦ Bake just until the bottoms of the cookies are barely golden brown, 15 to 20 minutes. Let the cookies cool completely on the baking sheet.

✦ Once the cookies are cool, carefully roll them around in the remaining 1 cup (100 g) powdered sugar until fully coated, and serve. Store cookies at room temperature in a sealed container for up to 5 days.

This is the iconic Mexican pink cake, known as cortadillo or pastel para niños in Mexico. If you can't decide which recipe in this book to start with, begin with this one. I have made this more times than I can count, and it always makes me say, "This is some good cake!" It is a simple but moist buttermilk and vanilla cake, with a fluffy pink vanilla frosting and rainbow sprinkles. It's one of my favorites because it's a simple but delicious recipe that never fails. She's my ride or die!

CORTADILLO
Mexican Pink Cake

Makes one 9 × 13-inch (23 × 33 cm) cake

FOR THE CAKE

2½ cups (312 g) unbleached all-purpose flour

2½ teaspoons baking powder

½ teaspoon Diamond Crystal kosher salt or ¼ teaspoon fine sea salt

¾ cup (12 tablespoons/170 g) unsalted butter, at room temperature

1¾ cups (350 g) granulated sugar

1½ teaspoons pure vanilla extract

3 large eggs

1⅓ cups (305 g) buttermilk

FOR THE BUTTERCREAM

1 cup (16 tablespoons/227 g) unsalted butter, at room temperature

1 teaspoon clear vanilla extract (see Tip on page 60)

½ teaspoon Diamond Crystal kosher salt or ¼ teaspoon fine sea salt

(continues)

✦ **Make the cake:** Preheat the oven to 350°F (180°C). Grease and line a 9 × 13-inch (23 × 33 cm) baking pan with a parchment sling so the two longer sides have a piece hanging over their edges to help with lifting later.

✦ In a medium bowl, whisk together the flour, baking powder, and salt and set aside.

✦ In a stand mixer fitted with the paddle, beat the butter and sugar on medium speed until light and fluffy and paler in color, about 2 minutes. Beat in the vanilla. Add the eggs, one at a time, beating well after each addition.

✦ Add one-third of the flour mixture and mix on low to incorporate. Add one-half of the buttermilk, followed by another one-third of the flour mixture. Add the final amount of buttermilk and the final amount of flour. Mix just until combined, then use a silicone spatula to scrape down the sides of the bowl to make sure everything's mixed in. Scrape the batter into the prepared pan, smooth it out, and bake until the cake is lightly golden brown and a toothpick or skewer inserted into the center of the cake comes out clean, 25 to 30 minutes.

✦ Let the cake cool in the pan before frosting.

✦ **Make the buttercream:** In a stand mixer fitted with the paddle, cream the butter with the vanilla and salt for 1 full minute at medium speed. Reduce the speed to low and add the powdered sugar ½ cup (50 g) at a time so you don't end up in a powdered sugar cloud. Keep the mixer on low speed and beat in the heavy cream to incorporate it, then increase the speed to medium-high for a full minute to make the buttercream nice and fluffy.

(continues)

4 cups (400 g) powdered sugar, sifted

¼ cup (57 g) heavy cream

Pink gel food coloring

Sprinkles

✦ Color the buttercream with gel food coloring, starting with a few drops and going up from there. Mix just until the color is incorporated.

✦ Spread the cake evenly with the buttercream and top with sprinkles. I like to place the cake back in the refrigerator for 30 to 45 minutes and wait for the buttercream to firm up for a clean cut, and an even better-tasting cake!

TIP: I use clear Mexican vanilla for the buttercream so as not to add a color to the frosting, but I use regular vanilla for the cake.

Tricolor polvorones are a type of sugar cookie in the shape of a triangle with a white side, a pink side, and a chocolate side that will melt in your mouth. I know it might be tempting to want to use butter for this recipe, but using butter will change this cookie. Stick to vegetable shortening for better consistency—and a cookie that will feel like it's straight out of the panadería.

POLVORONES TRICOLOR
Tricolored Sugar Cookies

Makes about 16 cookies

2½ cups (312 g) unbleached
  all-purpose flour

2½ cups (250 g) powdered sugar

1 teaspoon Diamond Crystal
  kosher salt or ½ teaspoon
  fine sea salt

1 teaspoon baking powder

1¼ cups (240 g) butter-flavored
  vegetable shortening

1 tablespoon pure vanilla extract

Red gel food coloring

2 tablespoons unsweetened
  cocoa powder

½ teaspoon ground cinnamon

FOR THE EGG WASH
1 large egg, whisked

✦ In a large bowl, whisk together the flour, powdered sugar, salt, and baking powder. Add the shortening to a stand mixer bowl and fit the mixer with the paddle. Cream the shortening on medium-low speed for a minute, then add the flour mixture ¼ cup (28 g) at a time. Once half of the flour mixture has been incorporated, add the vanilla extract. Divide the dough into 3 equal portions, each weighing about 269 g. Put the balls of dough in a bowl and cover them with plastic wrap to prevent them from drying out.

✦ Add one of the balls of dough to the mixer bowl and add a few drops of red food gel coloring and mix on medium-low speed until the coloring has been distributed equally. Scrape out the pink dough, pack it into a ball, and toss it back into the bowl with the other dough. Add another ball of white dough to the mixer and add the cocoa powder and cinnamon. Beat this together on medium speed until the cocoa powder has been equally distributed, about 1 minute. Pack into a ball.

✦ Roll a ball of dough between your hands to form a log 8 inches (20 cm) long and 1½ inches (2.5 cm) in diameter. Repeat with the other balls of dough. Place a long piece of plastic wrap over a large baking sheet and arrange 2 logs of dough side by side on top of it.

✦ Brush the top of the logs with the egg wash, then place the third log of dough on top to create a pyramid. Cover the cookie dough with plastic wrap, then use your hands to gently finish molding it into a long triangular log 2½ to 3 inches (6 to 7.5 cm) tall. Refrigerate the dough for 3 hours.

✦ Preheat the oven to 350°F (180°C), then line two 13 × 18-inch (33 × 45 cm) baking sheets with parchment paper.

✦ Transfer the chilled log of dough to a cutting board, then slice crosswise into 16 triangular cookies ½ inch (1.25 cm) thick. Place 8 cookies per baking sheet, then bake one sheet at a time. Bake until the cookies are puffed and risen, 10 to 12 minutes.

✦ Let cool on the baking sheet for 10 minutes before serving.

Polvorón is a catch-all name for many different cookies in Mexico, but in a panadería, you might recognize these polvorones as the big pink (or yellow or orange) sugar cookies that are rolled in sugar and baked until they've got tiny cracks all over. Since launching Chicano Eats, this has become my most popular recipe with reviews like "I used to get these at my local panadería, but have not seen any after moving. I figured I'd make them myself, so this recipe is a godsend! They taste better than the ones I used to buy. Thank you so much!" I know these cookies are going to become one of your favorites, too.

POLVORONES ROSAS
Pink Sugar Cookies

Makes 18 to 20 polvorones

4⅓ cups (541 g) unbleached
  all-purpose flour

2 teaspoons baking soda

1 teaspoon baking powder

¾ teaspoon Diamond Crystal
  kosher salt or heaping
  ¼ teaspoon fine sea salt

1¾ cups (336 g) butter-flavored
  vegetable shortening or lard

1½ cups (300 g) granulated sugar

1 tablespoon pure vanilla extract

2 large eggs

Gel food colorings

⅓ cup (67 g) cane sugar,
  to roll cookies in

✦ In a large bowl, whisk together the flour, baking soda, baking powder, and salt. Set aside.

✦ In a stand mixer fitted with the paddle, beat together the shortening, granulated sugar, and vanilla for 2 full minutes on medium speed, until light and fluffy. Add the eggs, one at a time, beating well after each addition. Turn the mixer to low and gradually add the flour mixture, 1 cup (128 g) at a time, until it's all fully combined.

✦ At this point, divide the dough into pieces for as many colors as you want (I usually stick to pink, yellow, and orange), then add food coloring and mix it into the dough with your hands or the stand mixer. Once the dough is dyed, wrap it in plastic and set it in the refrigerator to rest for 1 hour.

✦ Preheat the oven to 350°F (180°C), then line three 13 × 18-inch (33 × 45 cm) baking sheets with parchment paper.

✦ Scoop out ¼-cup (about 67 g) balls of dough (I just use a standard ice cream scoop) and roll them into a smooth ball before rolling in the cane sugar. Place 5 to 6 balls of dough on a baking sheet and flatten slightly with the back of a measuring cup, then sprinkle a bit more sugar on each cookie. Working in batches of one sheet at a time, bake the cookies until they have spread out and cracked but haven't browned at all, 12 to 14 minutes.

✦ Let the cookies cool for 5 minutes on the baking sheet before transferring them to a wire rack to cool completely.

Galletas con chochitos or galletas grageas—or "cookies con sprinkles" as I'd like to call them—are snappy butter cookies covered in sprinkles that are best enjoyed with a cup of Chocolate Caliente (page 200) or Champurrado (page 192)!

GALLETAS GRAGEAS
Mexican Sprinkle Cookies

Makes twenty cookies

2¼ cups (281) unbleached all-purpose flour

1 teaspoon baking powder

¾ teaspoon Diamond Crystal kosher salt or ¼ teaspoon fine sea salt

¾ cup (12 tablespoons/170 g) unsalted butter, at room temperature

¾ cup (150 g) sugar

2 large egg yolks

1 tablespoon pure vanilla extract

3 ounces (84 g) rainbow nonpareils or rainbow sprinkles

✦ In a large bowl, whisk together the flour, baking powder, and salt. Set aside.

✦ In a stand mixer fitted with the paddle, cream the butter and sugar on medium speed until fluffy and pale in color, about 2 minutes. Reduce the speed to low and add the egg yolks one at a time, beating well after each addition. Beat in the vanilla. Add the flour mixture 1 cup (125 g) at a time, until it's all fully combined.

✦ Pour the sprinkles into a small bowl, then use a 1½ tablespoon-size cookie scoop to scoop out 20 (30 g) equal-size balls of dough. Use your hands to roll the cookie dough into smooth balls, then dip and roll the dough balls in the sprinkles to get an even coat.

✦ Evenly space the cookie dough balls about 1 inch (2.5 cm) from one another on a large baking sheet lined with parchment paper. Cover the baking sheet with plastic wrap and refrigerate for 1 hour.

✦ Preheat the oven to 350°F (180°C). Once the cookie dough has chilled for an hour, bake for 22 to 26 minutes, until the cookies are lightly golden in color. Transfer them to a wire rack to cool for 10 to 15 minutes before serving.

Panque de nuez is a cool but simple girl who's an icon in the world of pan dulce. This is a classic Mexican pound cake sold as loaves or slices with a rich buttery crumb studded with pecans. My version comes with a sweet streusel to dress up the classic.

PANQUE DE NUEZ
Sweet Pecan Loaf

Makes one 9 × 5-inch (23 × 12.5 cm) loaf

FOR THE STREUSEL

¼ cup (31 g) unbleached all-purpose flour

2 tablespoons light brown sugar

¼ teaspoon ground cinnamon

Pinch of salt

¼ cup (27 g) chopped pecans

1 tablespoon (14 g) unsalted butter, at room temperature

FOR THE LOAF

1¾ cups (218 g) unbleached all-purpose flour

1 teaspoon baking powder

½ teaspoon Diamond Crystal kosher salt or ¼ teaspoon fine sea salt

¾ cup (172 g) buttermilk, at room temperature

3 large eggs, at room temperature

2 teaspoons pure vanilla extract

¾ cup (12 tablespoons/170 g) unsalted butter, at room temperature

1¼ cups (250 g) granulated sugar

¾ cup (81 g) chopped pecans

✦ **Make the streusel:** In a medium bowl, whisk together the flour, brown sugar, cinnamon, and salt. Stir in the pecans, then use your hands to incorporate the butter until you have a mixture that resembles wet sand. Set aside.

✦ **Make the loaf:** Preheat the oven to 350°F (180°C). Grease a 9 × 5-inch (23 × 12.5 cm) loaf pan, then make a sling by lining the pan with a strip of parchment across the width that overhangs the sides by at least 2 inches (5 cm) to make it easier to take the loaf out of the pan later.

✦ In a large bowl, whisk together the flour, baking powder, and salt. In a large measuring cup, whisk together the buttermilk, eggs, and vanilla. Set both aside.

✦ In a stand mixer fitted with the paddle, beat together the butter and granulated sugar on medium-high speed until the mixture is fluffy and pale in color, 2 minutes.

✦ Reduce the speed to low, then alternate adding the flour mixture and the buttermilk mixture, beginning and ending with the flour mixture. Scrape down the sides of the bowl, then beat the batter on medium speed for a full minute. Fold the chopped pecans into the batter.

✦ Pour the batter into the prepared pan, then sprinkle the streusel mixture on top of the batter.

✦ Bake until a toothpick inserted into the center of the loaf comes out clean, 1 hour to 1 hour 10 minutes. Let the loaf cool completely in the pan before slicing and serving.

Rebanadas, which means "slices" in Spanish, are slices of bread with a thin layer of butter on top and a sprinkle of sugar. I love the simplicity of the classic, but I like to take mine up a notch and top these fluffy slices of bread with a whipped honey butter and sprinkle of cinnamon!

REBANADAS

Makes about 12 slices

FOR THE LOAF

¼ cup (59 g) slightly hot water (100° to 110°F/38° to 43°C)

⅓ cup (67 g) sugar, plus 1 tablespoon

1 tablespoon active dry yeast

4 cups (500 g) unbleached all-purpose flour

¾ teaspoon Diamond Crystal kosher salt or a heaping ¼ teaspoon fine sea salt

½ cup (115 g) buttermilk

2 large eggs, at room temperature

½ cup (115 g) unsalted butter, at room temperature

FOR THE EGG WASH

1 large egg, whisked

FOR THE HONEY BUTTER

1 cup (16 tablespoons/227 g) unsalted butter, at room temperature

½ cup (168 g) honey, plus more to taste

1 teaspoon Diamond Crystal kosher salt or ½ teaspoon fine sea salt

1 teaspoon pure vanilla extract

Ground cinnamon, for serving

✦ **Make the loaf:** In a large measuring cup, stir the hot water and 1 tablespoon of the sugar together, then stir in the yeast. Let it sit for 10 minutes until foamy.

✦ In the bowl of a stand mixer, whisk together the flour, remaining ⅓ cup (67 g) sugar, and salt. Snap on the dough hook and turn the speed to low. Pour in the yeast mixture and beat to incorporate. Blend in the buttermilk. Add the eggs, one at a time, beating well after each addition. Add the butter. Gradually bump the speed up to medium and let the dough knead for about 2 minutes, until it comes together. Then bump up the speed to medium-high and let the dough knead for a final 4 minutes.

✦ Transfer to a large greased bowl and cover with plastic wrap. Let the dough sit in a warm dark place to rise and double in size, about 2 hours.

✦ Punch the dough down and let it rest for 5 minutes. Transfer to a lightly floured surface and roll the dough out into an 8 × 12-inch (20 × 30.5 cm) rectangle. With a long side of the rectangle facing you, roll the dough toward you to make a log 12 inches (30.5 cm) long, pinching the dough together at the seam. Line a 13 × 18-inch (33 × 45 cm) baking sheet with parchment. Place the log seam side down on the baking sheet. Lightly spritz a large piece of plastic wrap with nonstick cooking spray, then cover with plastic wrap and let it proof until doubled in size, about 45 minutes.

✦ Preheat the oven to 350°F (180°C).

✦ Brush the log of dough with the egg wash and bake until the top is brown and glossy, 32 to 35 minutes. Transfer to a wire rack to cool completely.

✦ **Make the honey butter:** In a stand mixer fitted with the whisk, whip together the butter, honey, salt, and vanilla until the mixture is smooth and fluffy, about 2 minutes. Taste for sweetness and add 1 to 2 tablespoons more honey if you'd like it sweeter.

✦ With a serrated knife, cut the loaf into about 12 slices 1½ inches (4 cm) thick. Serve each slice with 2 to 3 tablespoons of the honey butter and a pinch of ground cinnamon.

Pan de elote is one of the very few things my mom would bake for us every summer when sweet white corn was in season. The best way I can describe this is as a fusion between a pound cake and corn bread. It's sweet, dense, and creamy, and perfect on its own or with a dab of butter or with a drizzle of honey.

PAN DE ELOTE

**Makes one 9 × 5 inch
(23 × 12.5 cm) loaf**

2¼ cups (281 g) unbleached
  all-purpose flour

1½ teaspoons baking powder

1 teaspoon Diamond Crystal
  kosher salt or ½ teaspoon
  fine sea salt

2 cups (300 g) fresh sweet white
  or yellow corn kernels (from
  about 3 large ears corn)

1 (14-ounce/397 g) can
  sweetened condensed milk

¼ cup (59 g) whole milk

⅓ cup (66 g) sugar

2 teaspoons pure vanilla extract

3 large eggs

¾ cup (12 tablespoons/170 g)
  unsalted butter, melted

✦ Preheat the oven to 350°F (180°C). Grease a 9 × 5-inch (23 × 12.5 cm) loaf pan, then make a sling by lining the pan with a strip of parchment across the width that overhangs the sides by at least 2 inches (5 cm) to make it easier to take the loaf out of the pan later.

✦ In a large bowl, sift in the flour, then whisk in the baking powder, and salt.

✦ In a blender, combine the corn kernels, condensed milk, whole milk, sugar, and vanilla. Blend on medium-high speed for a minute, until you have a smooth puree. Pour the corn puree into a medium-sized bowl, then whisk in the eggs, one at a time, followed by the melted butter. Add the wet ingredients to the dry ingredients and whisk together just until combined and no traces of flour remain.

✦ Pour the batter into the loaf pan and bake until the top is golden brown and a toothpick inserted into the center comes out clean, 1 hour to 1 hour 15 minutes.

✦ Let the loaf cool in the pan completely before slicing.

Pan de muerto is typically enjoyed during the days leading up to Día de Muertos, which is observed November 1 through November 2. These sweet little rolls laced with aromatics like orange zest, cinnamon, cardamom, and ginger are used to represent those who have passed on. The rolls are topped with crossbones and a round ball to represent the skull, and sometimes they're covered with sesame seeds to represent the tears of the deceased souls who haven't been able to find peace. My recipe yields an incredibly soft spiced roll dusted with cinnamon sugar!

PAN DE MUERTO

Makes 6 rolls

FOR THE ROLLS

½ cup (118 g) whole milk

1 tablespoon active dry yeast

⅓ cup (67 g) sugar, plus
   1 tablespoon

4 cups (500 g) unbleached
   all-purpose flour

1½ teaspoons ground cinnamon

½ teaspoon ground ginger

½ teaspoon freshly grated
   nutmeg

½ teaspoon ground cardamom

½ teaspoon Diamond Crystal
   kosher salt or ¼ teaspoon
   fine sea salt

¼ teaspoon ground allspice

1 orange

2 large eggs, at room
   temperature

⅓ cup (76 g) unsalted butter,
   at room temperature

FOR THE EGG WASH

1 egg whisked with 1 tablespoon
   cold water

(continues)

✦ In the microwave, heat the milk to 100° to 110°F (38° to 43°C), 35 to 40 seconds. Mix in the yeast and the 1 tablespoon sugar. Set the yeast aside for 10 minutes until bubbling.

✦ Meanwhile, in the bowl of a stand mixer, whisk together the flour, remaining ⅓ cup (67 g) sugar, cinnamon, ginger, nutmeg, cardamom, salt, and allspice. Grate the zest of the orange into the stand mixer bowl, then juice the orange into a measuring cup to measure out ¼ cup (59 g) of orange juice. If the orange doesn't have enough juice, simply add a bit of water until it meets ¼ cup.

✦ Fit the stand mixer with the dough hook. Pour the yeast mixture into the bowl, turn the speed to low, and pour in the orange juice. Add the eggs, one at a time, beating well after each addition. Add the softened butter and let knead until the dough starts to come together into a ball, about 2 minutes, then gradually bump the speed up to medium and let knead for a final 4 minutes. Cover the bowl with plastic and let the dough rest in a dark and warm place until doubled in size, about 2 hours.

✦ Line two 13 × 18-inch (33 × 45 cm) half-sheet pans with parchment paper.

✦ Punch the dough down and let it rest for 5 minutes. Divide the dough into 8 equal portions (about 115 g each), and form into balls. Evenly space 6 of the balls on one baking sheet, then use your palm to flatten them.

✦ To form the crossbones, take the remaining 2 portions of dough and divide each one into 3 portions (about 39 g each), for a total of 6 small portions. You'll be using each portion to form the crossbones.

✦ For each skull and crossbone set, use one of the small dough portions. Pull off 5 grams of the dough and roll it into a smooth ball (the "skull") and place it on the empty lined sheet pan. Divide the remaining 34 grams

(continues)

FOR FINISHING

1 cup (200 g) sugar

½ teaspoon ground cinnamon

½ cup (8 tablespoons/115 g) unsalted butter, melted

of dough in two and roll each piece into a 6-inch (15 cm) snake with your hands. Lay a snake on the work surface, spread open your fingers, and roll with your fingertips so that some parts of the snake are lower than the others, to create a bone shape. Repeat this process with the remaining dough until you have six small balls and a set of crossbones for each roll. Place the skull and crossbone sets on the second baking sheet, lightly spritz two large pieces of plastic wrap with nonstick cooking spray, then loosely cover each baking sheet and place both baking sheets in a dark warm place to rise for 45 minutes.

✦ Meanwhile, preheat the oven to 350°F (180°C).

✦ Brush the risen rolls with the egg wash, then gently take the crossbones and crisscross them on top of each roll, gently brushing each piece with egg wash to hold them all together. Then place the little ball that represents the skull on top of the crossbones, making sure it's in the center of the crisscrossed bones.

✦ Bake until lightly golden brown, 16 to 18 minutes.

✦ Meanwhile, in a small bowl, stir together the sugar and cinnamon.

✦ Transfer the baked rolls to a wire rack to cool for 10 minutes. Brush each roll with melted butter, sprinkle with cinnamon sugar, and tap off any excess. Serve the rolls warm.

Pineapple upside-down cake, or volteado de piña, is one of my favorite American classics. For this recipe, I like to use a combination of pineapple juice and buttermilk, to infuse the cake with some tang and even more pineapple flavor, which pairs really well with the rich and buttery brown sugar and bourbon topping that drips down the sides of the cake. Make sure to opt for fresh pineapple for the topping; I found that using fresh pineapple gives a better flavor and consistency than canned.

VOLTEADO DE PIÑA
Fresh Pineapple Upside-Down Cake

Makes one 8-inch (20 cm) cake; serves 6 to 8

FOR THE TOPPING

¼ cup (4 tablespoons/57 g) unsalted butter

½ cup (104 g) light brown sugar

1½ tablespoons bourbon or spiced black rum

1 teaspoon pure vanilla extract

Pinch of salt

1 fresh pineapple

FOR THE BATTER

1⅓ cups (166 g) unbleached all-purpose flour

1½ teaspoons baking powder

¼ teaspoon Diamond Crystal kosher salt or ⅛ teaspoon fine sea salt

½ cup (8 tablespoons/115 g) unsalted butter, at room temperature

¾ cup (150 g) granulated sugar

2 tablespoons light brown sugar

½ cup (118 g) buttermilk

¼ cup (57 g) pineapple juice (see Note on page 79)

(continues)

✦ Preheat the oven to 350°F (180°C). Mist an 8-inch (20 cm) cake pan with cooking spray.

✦ **Make the topping:** In a medium saucepan, melt the butter completely. Remove from the heat and add the brown sugar, bourbon or rum, vanilla, and salt and whisk until smooth. Pour the mixture into the cake pan and use a silicone spatula to smooth it out evenly.

✦ Slice off the top and bottom of the pineapple, then use a knife to carefully remove the peel from the outside. Cut the pineapple into quarters, slicing from top to bottom, then lay each quarter on the cutting board and cut at an angle to remove the core. Slice half the pineapple into slices ¼ inch (6 mm) thick (see Note on page 79).

✦ Pat the slices with a paper towel so some of the moisture is absorbed, then arrange however you'd like over the butter and brown sugar topping. You should be able to cover the whole bottom nicely without overlapping the pineapple more than 2 slices deep. Set this aside.

✦ **Make the batter:** In a medium bowl, whisk together the flour, baking powder, and salt.

✦ In a stand mixer fitted with the paddle, beat together the butter and both sugars on medium speed until fluffy and pale in color, about 1 minute. In a large measuring cup, whisk together the buttermilk, pineapple juice, whole egg, egg yolk, and vanilla. With the mixer running, slowly and steadily pour the buttermilk mixture into the butter until everything has been fully incorporated.

✦ With the mixer on low, add the flour mixture ⅓ cup (42 g) at a time, then turn off the mixer and scrape down the sides. Mix the cake for another 30 seconds on medium speed. Scrape the cake batter into the cake pan and carefully smooth it out using an offset spatula, trying your best to not disturb the pineapple.

(continues)

1 large egg

1 large egg yolk

1 teaspoon pure vanilla extract

Vanilla ice cream, for serving

✦ Bake until a toothpick inserted into the center comes out clean, 45 to 55 minutes.

✦ Let the cake cool in the pan for exactly 10 minutes before inverting it onto a serving dish or cake stand; any longer and you risk all the upside-down portion sticking to the pan, leaving you with an ugly (but delicious) yellow cake. Serve warm or at room temperature with vanilla ice cream. Store leftover cake wrapped with plastic wrap in the refrigerator for up to 3 days.

NOTE: One of the issues with canned pineapple is it's too thick so it doesn't fully bake through. Using fresh pineapple and slicing it thinly guarantees it cooks perfectly and almost melts in your mouth with the cake. Since we only need half the pineapple, you can juice the other half for the juice needed in the cake batter if you're feeling ambitious.

Pastelitos de guayaba are flaky and buttery little pockets filled with cream cheese and guava paste. They're a Cuban pastry that is adored all over Latin America and are actually really easy to make! I like to sneak fresh lime juice and lime zest into the cream cheese filling to brighten it up and make the sweet and tropical notes in the guava paste pop.

PASTELITOS DE GUAYABA

Makes 6 pastries

8 ounces (227 g) full-fat cream cheese, at room temperature

Grated zest of 1 lime

1 tablespoon fresh lime juice

⅓ cup (67 g) sugar

Pinch of salt

1½ teaspoons pure vanilla extract

2 (225 g) sheets store-bought frozen puff pastry, thawed but still cold (see Tip)

6 ounces (170 g) guava paste

FOR THE EGG WASH

1 large egg whisked with 1 tablespoon cold water

✦ In a stand mixer fitted with the paddle, combine on low speed the softened cream cheese, lime zest, lime juice, sugar, salt, and vanilla. Gradually bump the speed up to medium and beat for 30 seconds, scrape down the sides, then beat for another 30 seconds, until smooth.

✦ Line a 13 × 18-inch (33 × 45 cm) half-sheet pan with parchment paper. Take both sheets of puff pastry and cut them into 12 rectangles 3 × 4½ inches (7.5 × 11.5 cm). If you happen to cut one a bit too short, just use a rolling pin to gently stretch it out. Place 6 of them on the baking sheet making sure to evenly space them to give them room to puff as they bake.

✦ Cut the guava paste into 12 equal rectangular slices (about 14 g each). Brush the egg wash around the outer ½ inch (1.25 cm) of each of the rectangles. Spoon or pipe 2 to 3 tablespoons of the cream cheese filling onto each rectangle, keeping it toward the center and about 1 inch (2.5 cm) away from the edge. Place 2 guava slices on top of the cream cheese. Once you've filled all 6 rectangles, take the remaining pieces of puff pastry and place them on top of each pastelito to cover. Use a fork to crimp around the edges to seal each one. Brush the tops with the egg wash and transfer them to the refrigerator to chill for 30 minutes before baking.

✦ Meanwhile, preheat the oven to 400°F (200°C).

✦ Bake the chilled pastelitos until they are puffed and golden, 20 to 22 minutes. Transfer to a wire rack to cool for at least 15 minutes before serving.

TIP: To thaw the puff pastry sheets, I like to unfold them and place them on a baking sheet lined with parchment paper to prevent them from sticking together and sticking to themselves. Thaw the sheets for about an hour at room temperature. You want them to still be cold but thawed enough that you can easily roll them out if you need to. If the puff pastry thaws too much, it becomes too soft and floppy and will be hard to work with.

Orejitas means "little ears," and these pastries are one of the easiest pan dulce recipes you can make and keep stocked in the freezer. They're flaky, buttery, covered in turbinado sugar, and named after the ear shape they take on after they're rolled and baked.

OREJITAS

Makes 9 to 10 pastries

¼ cup (4 tablespoons/57 g) unsalted butter, melted

½ teaspoon ground cinnamon

Pinch of salt

1 (225 g) sheet store-bought frozen puff pastry, thawed but still cold (see Tip)

6 tablespoons (78 g) turbinado sugar

✦ In a small bowl, whisk together the melted butter, cinnamon, and salt.

✦ Place the sheet of puff pastry on a work surface. Lightly brush one side of the sheet with half of the cinnamon butter, then sprinkle 3 tablespoons of the turbinado sugar evenly over it and use your hands or a rolling pin to gently press the sugar into the dough. Carefully flip the puff pastry, lightly brush the second side with the remaining cinnamon butter, then sprinkle the remaining 3 tablespoons turbinado sugar over evenly. Use your hands or a rolling pin to gently press the sugar onto this side of the dough.

✦ The puff pastry sheet should already be creased and divided into three sections from having been stored folded up. Rotate the sheet so the creases run horizontally. Take the bottom edge and fold it away from you twice to meet the bottom crease, then fold once more. Repeat this process with the top of the sheet, folding it toward you three times. There should be a small gap left in the middle. Fold both sides toward one another until they touch, as if you were closing a book. Transfer the finished dough to a small baking sheet and refrigerate for 30 minutes.

✦ Meanwhile, preheat the oven to 400°F (200°C). Line a 13 × 18-inch (33 × 45 cm) half-sheet pan with parchment paper.

✦ Slice the dough crosswise into 9 to 10 pieces 1 inch (2.5 cm) thick. Arrange the slices on the lined pan cut side up. Make sure to space them evenly, as they'll expand as they bake.

✦ Bake until they're puffed up and nice and golden, 16 to 18 minutes. Don't overbake or the sugar will overcaramelize and make them bitter.

TIP: To thaw the puff pastry sheets, I like to unfold them and place them on a baking sheet lined with parchment paper to prevent them from sticking together and sticking to themselves. Thaw the sheets for about an hour at room temperature. You want them to still be cold but thawed enough that you can easily roll them out if you need to. If the puff pastry thaws too much, it becomes too soft and floppy and will be hard to work with.

Rosca de Reyes, or King's Cake, is a traditional cake that we enjoy on January 6 (and in the days leading up to it), to celebrate Día de los Reyes Magos, or Three Kings' Day. This is a yeasted cake in the shape of a round or oval ring, with strips of a sweet streusel topping and dried fruits meant to represent the jewels of a crown. If you've never had it before, beware! There's usually a plastic doll representing baby Jesus hidden somewhere in the cake, and according to tradition, if you happen to get the slice with the baby in it, you have to host a tamal dinner on February 2 for Día de la Candelaria. If you happen to find the baby, head over to Chapter 5—I got you covered with the tamales!

ROSCA DE REYES
King's Cake

Makes 1 large ring cake

FOR THE CAKE

¼ cup (59 g) slightly hot water (100° to 110°F/38° to 43°C)

⅓ cup (67 g) sugar, plus 1 tablespoon

1 tablespoon active dry yeast

4 cups (500 g) unbleached all-purpose flour

1½ teaspoons ground cinnamon

1 teaspoon freshly grated nutmeg

1 teaspoon Diamond Crystal kosher salt or ½ teaspoon fine sea salt

½ cup (115 g) buttermilk, at room temperature

2 large eggs, at room temperature

⅓ cup (76 g) unsalted butter, at room temperature

(continues)

+ **Make the cake:** In a large measuring cup, stir the slightly hot water and 1 tablespoon of the sugar together, then stir in the yeast. Let the mixture sit for 10 minutes until bubbling and foamy.

+ In the bowl of a stand mixer, whisk together the flour, cinnamon, nutmeg, remaining ⅓ cup (67 g) sugar, and salt in a large bowl. Snap on the dough hook and turn the speed on to low. Pour in the yeast mixture and beat to incorporate. Beat in the buttermilk. Add the eggs, one at a time, beating well after each addition. Add the butter and let the dough knead until it comes together, about 2 minutes. Bump up the speed to medium and let the dough knead for a final 4 minutes.

+ Transfer to a large greased bowl and cover with plastic wrap. Let the dough sit in a warm dark place to rise and double in size, about 2 hours.

+ Punch the dough down and let it rest for 5 minutes. Line a 13 × 18-inch (33 × 46 cm) baking sheet with parchment paper. Transfer the dough to a lightly floured work surface and roll it out into a smooth rope 28 inches (70 cm) long. Form the dough rope into an oval on the lined baking sheet, then grab one end and use it to enclose the second end, pinching any seams to close. If you are hiding a plastic baby, press it into the dough at this time, making sure to pinch any seams closed.

+ Let the dough rest in a dark and warm place until doubled in size, 45 minutes to 1 hour.

+ **Meanwhile, make the topping:** In the bowl of a stand mixer, whisk together the powdered sugar, flour, baking powder, and salt. Snap on the paddle attachment, add the shortening and vanilla and beat on low speed until the dough starts to come together, about 30 seconds. Scrape the sides of the bowl and beat for a full minute, until the dough comes together in a smooth round ball. Cover with plastic wrap to prevent it from drying out.

(continues)

FOR THE TOPPING

¾ cup (75 g) powdered sugar, sifted

⅔ cup (84 g) unbleached all-purpose flour

¼ teaspoon baking powder

¼ teaspoon Diamond Crystal kosher salt or a pinch of fine sea salt

⅓ cup (64 g) butter-flavored vegetable shortening, cubed

1 tablespoon pure vanilla extract

FOR THE EGG WASH

1 large egg whisked with 1 tablespoon water

FOR SERVING

3 tablespoons granulated sugar

½ teaspoon ground cinnamon

¼ cup (4 tablespoons/57g) unsalted butter, melted

✦ About 30 minutes before the ring of dough is done proofing, preheat the oven to 350°F (180°C).

✦ Brush the ring with the egg wash. Divide the topping into 4 equal portions, then line a tortilla press with two squares of plastic (a 1-gallon resealable plastic bag cut into two pieces is perfect for this). Place one of the balls of dough and press down until you have a 5-inch (12.5 cm) round. Use a knife to carefully slice 2 strips 2 inches (5 cm) wide from the center. Carefully remove the remaining dough and return it to the remaining topping dough. Gently peel the 2 strips of dough onto your hand and drape them crosswise over the ring of dough (going from the inner edge to the outer edge of the ring). Space the strips 1 to 1½ inches (2.5 to 4 cm) apart. Repeat this process with the remaining balls of dough, then knead all the scraps of extra topping together to make more strips if you need them.

✦ Bake the cake until the internal temperature reaches about 200°F (93°C) and the outside is golden brown and glossy, 24 to 26 minutes. Let the cake cool completely on the baking sheet.

✦ **To serve:** In a small bowl, stir together the sugar and cinnamon. Brush the golden brown sections of the ring (in between the strips of topping) with melted butter and sprinkle cinnamon sugar over these sections.

The niño envuelto is a jelly roll that consists of a sponge cake rolled around different flavors of filling—usually a thin layer of jelly—and covered in shredded coconut. I like to use dulce de leche to fill mine as it pairs with shredded coconut the best, and I like to make thin sponge cake so you get a more swirly slice. There are a few options for the filling: You can make the recipe as is or go another route by using a thin layer of jam instead of the dulce de leche. Just make sure the jam is free of any large chunks of fruit so that rolling up the cake is as easy as possible.

NIÑO ENVUELTO
Jelly Roll

Serves 6

FOR THE BUTTERMILK CAKE

1 cup (125 g) unbleached all-purpose flour

1½ teaspoons baking powder

½ teaspoon Diamond Crystal kosher salt or ¼ teaspoon fine sea salt

4 large eggs

¾ cup (150 g) granulated sugar

⅓ cup (76 g) buttermilk

⅓ cup (75 g) neutral oil, like canola or avocado

1½ teaspoons pure vanilla extract

¼ teaspoon cream of tartar

2 tablespoons (24 g) powdered sugar

FOR ASSEMBLY

1 cup (226 g) dulce de leche

¾ cup (75 g) unsweetened finely shredded coconut

✦ **Make the buttermilk cake:** Preheat the oven to 350°F (180°C). Mist a 13 × 18-inch (33 × 46 cm) half-sheet pan with cooking spray and line the bottom with a piece of parchment paper.

✦ In a medium bowl, whisk together the flour, baking powder, and salt.

✦ Separate the eggs, placing the whites in the bowl of a stand mixer and the yolks in a large bowl. To the yolks, add the sugar, buttermilk, oil, and vanilla and whisk to combine the ingredients fully. Set aside.

✦ Snap the whisk attachment onto the stand mixer and whisk the egg whites on low until foamy, then add the cream of tartar, bump up the speed to medium-high, and beat until you've got stiff peaks, 2½ to 3 minutes. Check for this by turning off the mixer, dipping the tip of the whisk into the whites, and flipping it over. If the beaten egg whites stay standing straight up you've got stiff peaks; if they fall over continue to beat until firm enough, trying not to overwhip them, which would make them clumpy.

✦ Sift the flour mixture into the yolk mixture and whisk to combine everything evenly. Add about one-third of the beaten egg whites to the batter and mix it in, not being super careful; the goal here is just to lighten the batter enough to make folding the rest of the egg whites in easier. Once you've lightened the batter, add another one-third of the egg whites and carefully fold them in with a large silicone spatula, cutting into the middle of the mixture and scooping the batter up and over, then scraping the spatula around the inside of the bowl and repeating the process until the egg whites have been fully incorporated. Try not to be too aggressive or overmix so the egg whites don't deflate. Add the final third of the egg whites and repeat the folding process until the batter is evenly mixed.

(continues)

✦ Pour the batter into the prepared pan, pouring it evenly the best you can to make spreading it out easier. Use a large offset spatula to then spread it. Transfer the pan to the oven and bake just until a toothpick inserted comes out clean, 11 to 13 minutes. Try not to overbake, as that can lead to the cake being dry and cracking too much when you go to roll it up.

✦ Pull the cake from the oven and immediately cover it with a kitchen towel. Let it sit covered for 10 minutes (no longer; see Note). After 10 minutes, the top of the cake will be slightly sticky to the touch, so carefully remove the towel and dust the cake with the powdered sugar, making sure to dust evenly. Rotate the sheet pan so a short end is facing you. Starting from the top edge, carefully roll the cake toward you. Let the cake sit rolled up for 10 minutes.

✦ **To assemble:** Unroll the cake. Take half of the dulce the leche and use an offset spatula to spread it over the top of the cake in a thin even layer. Evenly sprinkle with the coconut and use your hand to press it into the dulce de leche to help it stick.

✦ Place a large sheet of parchment over the top of the cake, then place a second 13 × 18-inch (33 × 46 cm) sheet pan over the cake and carefully flip to invert the cake so the coconut layer is now on the bottom. Inverting the cake onto a second baking sheet makes it easier to flip, and will help you have better control of the cake once it comes time to roll it. Gently peel off the piece of parchment the cake baked on, then spread the rest of the dulce de leche in another thin layer over the cake. Roll up the cake toward you, then let it cool completely before slicing.

✦ To serve, use a serrated bread knife to cut the log into slices 2 inches (5 cm) thick.

NOTE: Make sure to assemble the cake while it's warm. It'll make the cake easier to work with and roll, as well as help spread the dulce de leche much easier. If you let it cool too much you run the risk of the cake cracking when you go to roll it.

Buñuelos de viento are the thin crispy fritters covered in cinnamon sugar that we get to enjoy during the holidays, and they're made with a rosette iron so you can make them in all sorts of shapes and sizes. You can typically find Mexican rosette irons (called buñueleras) during the holidays at Mexican grocery stores, or online at sites like Etsy and Amazon year-round!

BUÑUELOS DE VIENTO

Makes about 24 buñuelos

FOR THE BUÑUELOS
2 large eggs

1¼ cups (295 g) whole milk

**2 tablespoons neutral oil,
   like canola or avocado**

1 teaspoon pure vanilla extract

**1½ cups (187 g) unbleached
   all-purpose flour**

**½ teaspoon Diamond Crystal
   kosher salt or ¼ teaspoon
   fine sea salt**

¼ teaspoon baking powder

2 tablespoons sugar

1 teaspoon ground cinnamon

FOR FRYING
6 cups (1.42 liters) vegetable oil

FOR THE SPICED SUGAR COATING
1¼ cups (250 g) sugar

1½ teaspoons ground cinnamon

¼ teaspoon ground ginger

✦ In a large bowl, whisk together the eggs, milk, oil, and vanilla until just combined. In another large bowl, combine the flour, salt, baking powder, sugar, and cinnamon. Slowly pour the wet ingredients into the dry mixture, constantly whisking until the liquid has been fully incorporated and the batter is smooth.

✦ Pour 4 inches (10 cm) of oil into a deep skillet or dutch oven and bring to 350°F (180°C).

✦ **Meanwhile, make the spiced sugar coating:** In a medium bowl, whisk together the sugar, cinnamon, and ginger. Have at the ready.

✦ When the oil is up to temperature, place the rosette iron in the oil for 5 minutes. Take the rosette iron out of the oil, let it drain for a second, then carefully dip the rosette iron halfway into the batter. (If you completely submerge the rosette into the batter, the buñuelo will enclose your iron once you dip it into the oil and won't release.) The iron needs to be hot enough so when you dip it into the batter, it sizzles. If the iron isn't hot enough and you don't hear a strong crackle and sizzle, the batter will stick to the iron when it's submerged in the hot oil and won't release the buñuelo.

✦ Place the rosette iron back into the oil and gently shake until the buñuelo releases into the oil. Fry for 20 to 30 seconds, then flip over and fry another 20 to 30 seconds, until the buñuelo is golden and crispy. Carefully transfer it to the spiced sugar coating and toss until coated. After making 4 or 5 buñuelos, make sure to let the rosette rest in the hot oil for 1 to 2 minutes, so it gets hot again.

✦ To store the buñuelos, make sure they are completely cool, then store in a large airtight container.

POSTRES

I have to confess, I have a big sweet tooth. I'm the type of person who always has something sweet planned after dinner because after a long day of work, a sweet something like creamy arroz con leche just helps me melt my troubles away. This is one of my favorite chapters in this book because a few of these recipes have been with me since the beginning, when I first launched Chicano Eats. I know I shouldn't be picking favorites, but you're going to run into my dulce de leche brownies—fudgy brownies laced with a glossy orange ribbon of dulce de leche that I used to sell at Markets in LA, which my husband, Billy, helped me perfect. They were always the first to sell out! You're also going to find another favorite, the Chicano Eats chocolate chip cookie. Just look to your left—isn't she beautiful? She's a cookie studded with shiny, gooey pools of chocolate so reflective you might even be able to use them to check your lip gloss. If your family is anything like mine, you're going to find yourself baking these cookies often!

DESSERTS

When I first started Chicano Eats, people would always ask me if I sold any of the sweet treats I'd share online, and this immediately sparked the idea to sell baked goods at markets in LA. My husband, Billy, had already developed the recipe for this brownie, and we knew we could bake them in a large quantity using his recipe. At our first event, the brownies were gone within thirty minutes—and someone even special-ordered a half-sheet pan for her boyfriend's birthday for the following week because he had eaten both the brownies she bought and loved them. At my next events, everyone would come up and ask for these brownies, and it was then that we were sure they were a hit. This is the same recipe that Billy knocked out of the park, just scaled down.

An added note from Billy: I know it might seem extra to separate eggs and use a double boiler to make brownies, but in the end it produces exactly what Esteban and I think are the perfect fudgy brownie with just a kiss of cakiness. The bonus of having that kiss sealed with what looks like lip gloss on top of the brownies in the form of a glossy layer of dulce de leche is the jewel in the crown of a perfect dessert. Also it's technically a one-bowl (plus maybe a tiny bowl) baked good, which means less mess so it cancels out any hassle you might have. Simple math!

DULCE DE LECHE BROWNIES

Makes 9 large brownies

1 cup (200 g) sugar

2 large eggs

⅔ cup (110 g) dark or semisweet chocolate chips

½ cup (8 tablespoons/115 g) unsalted butter, cubed

½ teaspoon Diamond Crystal kosher salt or ¼ teaspoon fine sea salt

½ cup (150 g) dulce de leche or cajeta

1 teaspoon pure vanilla extract

⅔ cup (60 g) Dutch process cocoa powder

⅔ cup (83 g) unbleached all-purpose flour

+ Preheat the oven to 350°F (180°C). Mist an 8-inch (20 cm) square baking pan with cooking spray. Line the pan with a piece of parchment so two sides stick over the edges of the pan.

+ **Create a makeshift double boiler:** Bring 1 inch (2.5 cm) of water to a simmer in a saucepan and find a bowl that can sit partially in the pan without touching the water. To that bowl (not over the water yet), add the sugar. Separate the eggs, add the whites to the bowl with the sugar, and set the yolks aside for later.

+ Set the bowl over the simmering water and whisk to combine the ingredients, then stir occasionally until the sugar has mostly dissolved and the mixture has loosened and warmed up. Remove the bowl from the saucepan and add half the chocolate chips, the butter, and salt. Whisk to make sure everything is combined and let it sit for 5 minutes to let the residual heat melt the chocolate and butter.

+ While the chocolate and butter melt, add the dulce de leche to a bowl and microwave in 30-second bursts, stirring after each, until the dulce de leche has just barely been warmed through and is easier to pour and swirl.

+ Stir the chocolate mixture to make sure everything is melted and evenly combined. Whisk in the vanilla with the reserved egg yolks, then sift in the cocoa powder and flour. Use a silicone spatula to fold together everything just until the flour and cocoa powder have disappeared. Fold in the rest of the chocolate chips.

(continues)

+ Scrape the batter into the prepared baking pan and carefully spread it out evenly with an offset spatula. Drop the warmed dulce de leche in 5 even dollops, one in each corner and one in the center, then use the offset spatula to carefully swirl the batter and dulce de leche together.

+ Bake until the brownies have puffed slightly and there's just the tiniest jiggle when you carefully shake the pan, about 20 minutes.

+ Let the brownies cool completely in the pan, then wrap tightly and refrigerate for 1 hour or so to let them fully set.

+ Cut into 9 squares and serve. Store leftover brownies in the refrigerator.

For my take on the empanada, I decided to create a turnover filled with diced apples covered in dulce de leche and nestled in a tangy bed of cream cheese filling that is then deep-fried and rolled in cinnamon sugar. These empanadas taste like heaven, and each bite transports me to the fair. Make sure you're using a thermometer to keep the temperature of the oil in check so the dough cooks properly.

CARAMEL APPLE
CHEESECAKE EMPANADAS

Makes 12 empanadas

FOR THE APPLE FILLING

2 cups (300 g) diced peeled Honeycrisp apples (about 2 large apples)

2 tablespoons (28 g) unsalted butter

1 tablespoon cornstarch

¼ cup (75 g) dulce de leche

1 teaspoon ground cinnamon

⅛ teaspoon ground allspice

⅛ teaspoon salt

FOR THE EMPANADA DOUGH

2½ cups (312 g) unbleached all-purpose flour

1½ teaspoons Diamond Crystal kosher salt or ¾ teaspoon fine sea salt

¾ teaspoon baking powder

¾ cup (177 g) hot water

⅓ cup (69 g) butter-flavored vegetable shortening, melted

(continues)

✦ **Make the filling:** In a medium saucepan, combine the apples, ¼ cup (59 g) water, and the butter. Cover and warm over medium-low heat for 5 minutes, just to heat up the mixture and evaporate some of the water.

✦ Meanwhile, mix together the cornstarch and 1 tablespoon water to make a slurry.

✦ Add the dulce de leche, cinnamon, allspice, salt, and cornstarch slurry to the apples. Once the mixture starts to bubble, cook for a full minute to activate the cornstarch, then transfer the apple filling to a small bowl to cool completely. The apple filling can be made 1 day ahead.

✦ **Make the empanada dough:** In the bowl of a stand mixer, whisk together the flour, salt, and baking powder. Snap on the dough hook attachment and turn the speed on to low. Slowly pour in the hot water. Once fully incorporated, pour in the melted shortening. Gradually bump the speed up to medium-high and let the dough knead until it comes together into a smooth ball, about 5 minutes.

✦ Cover the bowl with plastic wrap and let sit for 20 minutes to let the dough fully hydrate.

✦ **Meanwhile, make the cream cheese filling:** In a stand mixer fitted with the paddle, beat together the cream cheese, sugar, and vanilla bean paste on medium speed until the mixture is evenly combined, about 30 seconds.

✦ **Make the cinnamon sugar:** In a wide shallow dish, combine the sugar and cinnamon. Set aside.

✦ Divide the dough into 12 equal balls (about 45 g each). Use a rolling pin to roll them into thin 7-inch (18 cm) rounds. The best way to get a perfect round is to roll the dough, then turn it, roll, then turn, to make sure the pressure is being distributed equally.

(continues)

FOR THE CREAM CHEESE FILLING

8 ounces (227 g) cream cheese, at room temperature

¼ cup (50 g) sugar

1 teaspoon vanilla bean paste

FOR THE CINNAMON SUGAR

½ cup (100 g) sugar

1 teaspoon ground cinnamon

FOR FRYING

About 1 quart (1 liter) neutral oil, such as canola or vegetable

✦ **To assemble the empanadas (see Note):** Place a heaping tablespoon of both the apple filling and the cream cheese filling on one side of a round of dough, then dip your finger in water and run it along the edge of the round and fold the other side of the dough over to make a half-moon. Use a fork to crimp down the edges to seal. Place the empanadas on a parchment-lined baking sheet.

✦ **Fry the empanadas:** Pour 4 inches (10 cm) of oil into a medium stockpot and heat to 360°F (182°C). Line a baking sheet with paper towels.

✦ Working in batches of 2 or 3 (to not overcrowd the pot), lower the empanadas into the pot and cook until golden brown on both sides, 1 to 2 minutes per side. Transfer to the paper towels. Let them cool for 1 minute before carefully placing them in the cinnamon sugar and turning them over a couple of times to fully coat. Let cool for about another 5 minutes before serving to make sure the filling isn't too hot.

NOTE: A really helpful tool for making empanadas is a 5-inch (12.5 cm) empanada press, a round mold hinged in the center. You lay a round of dough over the mold, add the filling, moisten the edges of the dough, and close the two sides of the press together, which also crimps the dough to seal.

Mastering the classic caramel flan took me a while, but I got there! The hardest part about making flan is making sure you don't let the caramel darken too much or it'll taste bitter. When you're making the caramel, don't stir, or it will crystallize. Swirl the pan occasionally, especially once it starts to develop some color, and let the pan do all of the work. I like to use half-and-half in my flan because it yields a smoother and creamier texture. I bake it at a lower temperature to make sure it doesn't overbake and end up looking like Swiss cheese.

CLASSIC CARAMEL FLAN

Serves 8 to 10

FOR THE CARAMEL

1 cup (200 g) sugar

FOR THE FLAN

1½ cups (354 g) half-and-half

3 large eggs

1 (14-ounce/397 g) can sweetened condensed milk

2 teaspoons pure vanilla extract

Pinch of salt

✦ Preheat the oven to 300°F (150°C). Mist an 8-inch (20 cm) round cake pan with cooking spray.

✦ **Make the caramel:** In a medium saucepan, combine the sugar and ¼ cup (59 g) water and set over low heat. Increase the heat to medium and cook, occasionally swirling the pan to distribute the caramelized sugar—do not stir or the sugar will seize and crystalize—until the mixture is amber in color, 8 to 12 minutes. As soon as all the sugar has turned an amber color, quickly and carefully pour the caramel into the prepared cake pan. Let this cool for 5 minutes.

✦ **Make the flan:** In a blender, combine the half-and-half, eggs, condensed milk, vanilla, and salt and blend until smooth, 20 to 30 seconds.

✦ Place the cake pan in a larger shallow metal baking dish like a roasting pan. Pour the flan into the cake pan and cover the cake pan tightly with foil. Fill the larger baking dish with warm or hot water to come halfway up the side of the cake pan.

✦ Bake until the outer rim of the custard is firm but the center still has some jiggle to it, 1 hour 15 minutes to 1 hour 30 minutes. Remove the cake pan from the water bath, then remove the foil completely and let cool at room temperature for about 1 hour. Place the foil back onto the cake pan and refrigerate until completely cool and set, at least 4 hours.

✦ When you're ready to serve, run a thin sharp knife around the edge of the cake pan to make sure the flan doesn't stick, then place a plate on top and quickly flip it over to invert. Lift off the cake pan and serve.

This recipe incorporates brown butter to add some nuttiness, two kinds of chocolate, and grated Mexican chocolate that melts into the dough, adding a kiss of cinnamon to make these cookies even more special. I like to buy bars of bittersweet and milk chocolate that I can chop myself, which give larger pools of chocolate in the finished cookie, but if you prefer the look and vibe of a classic chocolate chip cookie, go with chocolate chunks or chips.

THE CHICANO EATS CHOCOLATE CHIP COOKIE

Makes 36 cookies

1 cup (16 tablespoons/227 g) unsalted butter

3 cups (375 g) unbleached all-purpose flour

1 teaspoon baking soda

1 teaspoon baking powder

1 teaspoon Diamond Crystal kosher salt or ½ teaspoon fine sea salt

1½ cups (312 g) light brown sugar

½ cup (70 g) grated Mexican chocolate (from about 1 tablet)

2 tablespoons granulated sugar

2 large eggs, cold

1 tablespoon pure vanilla extract

1 cup bittersweet chocolate chunks or chips (see Note on page 104)

1 cup milk chocolate chunks or chips (see Note on page 104)

✦ Preheat the oven to 375°F (190°C).

✦ In a medium stainless steel saucepan or skillet, melt 8 tablespoons (115 g) of the butter over medium heat. Wait for it to start fizzling and foaming, stirring occasionally with a silicone spatula to make sure nothing burns. As the butter fizzles the milk solids toast/brown, giving the finished product a hint of toffee flavor. Once the fizzling stops it's time to start checking for doneness. The melted liquid should be a golden color and there should be golden-brown toasted milk solids on the bottom of the pan. Once you've achieved this, place the brown butter in a heatproof medium bowl, making sure to scrape all the flavorful browned bits off the bottom of the pan along with it. Add the remaining 8 tablespoons (115 g) butter to the browned butter while it's still hot so it can melt as well as help cool down the browned butter. Set this aside to cool for 15 to 20 minutes, stirring occasionally to make sure the second half of the butter fully melts.

✦ In a large bowl, whisk together the flour, baking soda, baking powder, and salt. Set aside.

✦ Once the melted butter has cooled to the touch, whisk in the brown sugar, grated Mexican chocolate, and granulated sugar until all combined. Add the eggs and vanilla and whisk the mixture until smooth.

✦ Add the wet ingredients all at once to the flour mixture in the large bowl and use a silicone spatula to scrape all the bits from the bowl where the butter was and mix everything together into a cohesive dough. Once almost all the flour has been mixed in, add the chopped chocolate or chocolate chips and stir just until they are evenly distributed; try not to overmix. You can also use a stand mixer with the paddle attachment for this step if you're finding it difficult to stir by hand.

(continues)

✦ Use a 1½-tablespoon cookie scoop to scoop out the dough while it's still soft and place the rough balls on a plate or in a container with a tight-fitting lid. This makes rolling and baking in the final stages much easier than trying to scoop cold cookie dough. When all the dough has been scooped out, wrap the plate tightly with plastic wrap or close the container and refrigerate for at least 1 hour and up to 2 days so the dough can rest and the flavors can intensify.

✦ Line a couple of large baking sheets with parchment paper.

✦ Take the scoops of dough and roll them into smooth balls and place 8 cookies on a baking sheet spaced 2 inches (5 cm) apart. Plant a few extra pieces of chocolate on top of each ball if you want an Instagram cookie moment. Baking one sheet at a time (see Tip), bake just until the dough has turned golden brown but still looks a little underbaked, 8 to 9 minutes.

✦ Let the cookies cool on the baking sheet for 5 minutes, then carefully move them to a wire cooling rack. Once they cool completely at room temperature, the cookies can be stored in a tightly sealed container to preserve freshness for up to 3 days.

NOTE: I haven't included weight for the chocolate chips in this recipe because it varies for the different brands of chocolate chips and chunks. With a 1-cup measuring cup to gauge the volume, measure out 2 cups total of your favorite high-quality chocolate and/or chip. I prefer an equal mix of milk and bittersweet chocolate. If you want the extra Insta-worthy decoration, be sure to have extra chocolate on hand.

TIP: If you want to form the cookies and freeze for baking later, place the balls of rested dough in a resealable freezer bag and freeze in a single layer. Frozen cookie dough can be baked straight from the freezer. There is no need to thaw it—just add an extra minute or two of baking time!

These bars are the Chicano Eats take on barritas, or snappy cookies in the shape of a bar, with a thin line of strawberry or pineapple jam (making them look a bit like Fig Newtons!). My bars are a beautiful cross between a slice of pie and a shortbread cookie, with a sweet strawberry-guava filling. Most guava pastes you find in the Mexican supermarkets are free of seeds and peels, but if the only option available has seeds, combine 10 ounces (283 g) with 3 tablespoons water, then strain the mixture through a fine-mesh sieve to get rid of seeds and pulp before measuring out the amount you need for the recipe.

STRAWBERRY GUAVA SHORTBREAD BARS

Makes 16 squares

FOR THE PASTRY

1½ cups (187 g) unbleached all-purpose flour

½ cup (100 g) sugar

½ teaspoon baking powder

¼ teaspoon Diamond Crystal kosher salt or ⅛ teaspoon fine sea salt

½ cup (8 tablespoons/115 g) unsalted butter, very cold (see Tip on page 107)

3 tablespoons sour cream

FOR THE STRAWBERRY-GUAVA FILLING

5 ounces (142 g) seedless guava paste

1 pound (455 g) strawberries, hulled and finely chopped (about 2 heaping cups)

1 tablespoon sugar

2 tablespoons cornstarch

Pinch of salt

✦ **Make the pastry:** Preheat the oven to 375°F (190°C). Coat an 8-inch (20 cm) square baking dish with cooking spray and place a piece of parchment so it covers the bottom and hangs over the edge of two sides of the pan.

✦ In a large bowl, mix together the flour, sugar, baking powder, and salt with a fork just until it's roughly combined. Grate the butter on the large holes of a box grater directly into the dry mixture. Once all the butter has been grated in, use your hands to toss the butter in the mixture and then squeeze it all together to break up the butter and start forming something resembling sand. Once you've broken down the butter to nothing larger than a pea, add the sour cream and use your fork to start the mixing process, then switch to your hands to fully incorporate. The easiest way to do this is just squeeze the mixture until the dough starts to hold shape. The mixture will look crumbly in the bowl but that's exactly what you're after.

✦ Measure out 1 cup (135 g) of the crumbled pastry and set aside. Spread the rest of the crumbled pastry in an even layer over the bottom of the prepared pan and use your hands to firmly press it in to make a solid base for the bars. Set the pan and the reserved topping in the refrigerator while you make the filling.

✦ **Make the strawberry-guava filling:** Roughly chop or break up the guava paste and add to a microwave-safe medium bowl. Add 1 tablespoon water. Microwave for 30 seconds, then carefully remove the bowl and whisk the mixture together until smooth. If it's having trouble breaking down, just heat it up for another 30 seconds and whisk again. (Alternatively, chop the guava paste up more finely and place it in a small bowl, add 1 tablespoon boiling water, then quickly cover with plastic wrap and let it sit for 15 minutes. This should help steam and soften the paste to get the consistency you're looking for.)

(continues)

✦ In a medium bowl, mix together the strawberries, sugar, cornstarch, and salt. Add the guava paste and stir to make sure everything is evenly combined.

✦ Spread the strawberry-guava filling over the pastry base in the pan, then sprinkle the reserved pastry over the top by squeezing a handful and breaking it up as you sprinkle, which will ultimately show more of the filling and give a prettier bar in the end.

✦ Bake until the pastry is nice and lightly golden brown and the filling has started to bubble up, 30 to 35 minutes. Make sure you don't remove the bars before the filling has bubbled because that is an indication that the cornstarch has been activated and the bars will set properly.

✦ Set the bars on a wire rack to cool completely in the pan before covering them with plastic wrap or foil and placing in the refrigerator to fully set. This final rest in the refrigerator is important to not only the flavor but also the texture of the bars.

✦ When you're ready to serve, just lift the bars out of the pan using the parchment sling and cut into 2-inch (5 cm) squares. Store leftovers in the refrigerator for up to 2 days.

TIP: I like to leave the butter in the freezer for 15 to 20 minutes.

Every time I tested this recipe, my kitchen would fill with the sweet and creamy scent of vanilla and cinnamon, instantly transporting me back to my mom's kitchen. Every. Single. Time. I kept this recipe as simple and traditional as possible, just with the addition of vanilla bean paste because this is my go-to recipe when I'm looking to treat myself with something comforting, and the addition of vanilla bean paste just makes it feel expensive!

ARROZ CON LECHE

Serves 4 to 6

1 cup long-grain rice

3 cups (708 g) whole milk

1 (14-ounce/397 g) can sweetened condensed milk

1½ teaspoons vanilla bean paste or pure vanilla extract

1 (4-inch/10 cm) stick cinnamon

Ground cinnamon, for serving

✦ In a medium saucepan, combine the rice and 1¾ cups (413 g) water and bring to a boil over medium heat. Cover, reduce the heat to low, and cook for 15 minutes. After 15 minutes, remove from the heat and let the rice steam for 15 minutes. Uncover and let cool for 5 minutes, then use a fork to fluff the rice.

✦ Stir in the whole milk, condensed milk, and vanilla. Add the cinnamon stick and use a silicone spatula to combine. Set over medium-low heat, bring to a simmer, and cook until it starts to thicken, about 20 minutes. Remove from the heat; the rice pudding will thicken as it cools.

✦ If you'd like to serve it warm, set aside and let it cool for 10 to 15 minutes. Otherwise, let it cool completely, cover, and let it chill in the refrigerator. Serve with a sprinkling of cinnamon.

This is the horchata tiramisu from my website in its best and final evolution. It's another one of the most popular recipes from the blog, which I updated once before, but in this version, she's got a point! She's an icon, she's a legend, and she IS the moment! This tiramisu features a fluffy mascarpone horchata filling with an airy horchata chiffon cake and an horchata espresso soak. The horchata used for this recipe needs to be a good, sweet milky horchata. If you'd like to make the horchata from scratch, I've got a recipe for Classic Horchata in my first cookbook, *Chicano Eats*, but you can also order a large horchata from your favorite taquería. Just make sure that as soon as you get it home you scoop out any ice to prevent the drink from getting too watered down.

HORCHATA TIRAMISU

Serves 6 to 8

FOR THE HORCHATA CHIFFON CAKE

1½ cups (187 g) unbleached all-purpose flour

1½ teaspoons baking powder

1½ teaspoons ground cinnamon

5 large eggs

1 cup (200 g) sugar

⅔ cup (157 g) horchata

⅓ cup (74 g) neutral oil, like canola or avocado

1½ teaspoons pure vanilla extract

½ teaspoon Diamond Crystal kosher salt or ¼ teaspoon fine sea salt

¼ teaspoon cream of tartar

FOR THE CAKE SOAK

¾ cup (177 g) horchata

¼ cup (59 g) freshly brewed espresso (see Tips on page 112)

(continues)

✦ **Make the horchata chiffon cake:** Preheat the oven to 350°F (180°C). Coat a 13 × 18-inch (33 × 46 cm) half-sheet pan with cooking spray and line the bottom with a piece of parchment paper.

✦ In a medium bowl, whisk together the flour, baking powder, and cinnamon. Set aside.

✦ Separate the eggs, placing the whites in the bowl of a stand mixer and the yolks in a large bowl. To the yolks, add the sugar, horchata, oil, vanilla, and salt. Whisk to combine the ingredients fully together. Set aside.

✦ Set the mixer bowl on the stand mixer and snap on the whisk. Whisk the egg whites on low until foamy, then add the cream of tartar and bump up the speed to medium-high and beat until you've got stiff peaks. Check for this by turning off the mixer and dipping the tip of the whisk into the whites and flipping it over. If the beaten egg whites stay standing straight up you've got stiff peaks; if they fall over, continue to beat until firm enough, trying not to overwhip them, which makes them clumpy.

✦ Sift the flour mixture into the yolk mixture and whisk to combine everything evenly. Then fold in the egg whites: Add one-third of the egg whites to the batter and mix it in, not being super careful, as the goal here is just to lighten the batter enough to make folding the rest of the egg whites in easier. Once you've lightened the batter, add another one-third of the egg whites and carefully fold them in with a large silicone spatula, cutting into the middle of the mixture and scooping the batter up and over, then scraping the spatula around the inside of the bowl and repeating the process until the egg whites have been fully incorporated. Try not to be too aggressive or overmix so the egg whites don't deflate. Add the final third of the egg whites and repeat the folding process until the batter is evenly mixed.

✦ Pour the batter into the prepared pan, as evenly as you can to make spreading it out easier. Use an offset spatula to evenly spread it the best you can. Bake the cake until it's just starting to turn golden brown on top and a toothpick inserted into the center comes out clean, 17 to 20 minutes. Set the cake aside to cool completely in the pan.

(continues)

FOR THE HORCHATA CREAM

1 pound (455 g) mascarpone cheese, cold (see Tips)

⅔ cup (157 g) horchata, cold

½ cup (114 g) heavy cream, cold

⅓ cup (67 g) sugar

2 tablespoons black rum, hazelnut liqueur, or coffee liqueur

½ teaspoon ground cinnamon

1 teaspoon pure vanilla extract

Pinch of kosher salt

FOR FINISHING

1 tablespoon unsweetened cocoa powder

✦ **Meanwhile, make the cake soak:** In a liquid measuring cup (to help make sure it's divided evenly as you use it), combine the horchata and espresso. Set aside.

✦ **Make the horchata cream:** In a stand mixer fitted with the whisk, add the mascarpone, and beat on low speed, then pour in the horchata, cream, sugar, rum, cinnamon, vanilla, and salt and continue beating for about 30 more seconds to combine. Bump the speed up to medium and whip until the mixture looks light and fluffy, 3 to 4 minutes. If you like a thicker set tiramisu, whip until the mixture is much thicker and fluffier, 4 to 5 minutes. Not all mascarpone whips up the same, softer mascarpone could take 10 to 15 minutes to reach soft peaks.

✦ Once all of the components are ready to go, assemble the tiramisu. Take a 2-quart (2-liter) square or oval baking dish and trace the bottom onto a piece of parchment paper. Cut out the tracing and use it as a guide to carve out two cake layers from the larger sheet cake.

✦ Once you have both layers carved out, evenly spread about a third of the horchata cream on the bottom of the baking dish. Place a layer of cake bottom side up on top. The bottom of the cake will absorb more liquid, so it is facing up for the soak. Carefully spoon half of the horchata espresso soak over the cake layer, making sure to use the full ½ cup (120 g). Scoop out half of the remaining horchata cream over the soaked cake layer and evenly smooth it out. Add the second cake layer bottom side up and spoon on the remaining espresso soak. Top with the rest of the horchata cream, which should come right up to the top of your baking dish or close to it. Smooth out the horchata cream as best as you can, then place a layer of plastic wrap directly on the surface and refrigerate to set. This should ideally sit 6 to 8 hours for all of the flavors and textures to get just right, but 4 hours works if you're in a hurry.

✦ Remove the plastic wrap and before serving, dust with a light even layer of cocoa powder.

TIPS: A quad shot of espresso from your local coffee shop should be the perfect amount.

When you make the horchata cream, grab the ingredients directly from the fridge so that they are cold. If the mascarpone or horchata is at room temperature, there's a high risk the mixture could curdle and not whip together properly.

My family is from the state of Colima, Mexico, which is known for producing and exporting key limes, and this is why I love the smell of citrus and the tart kiss of limes so much. This recipe is not for an ordinary key lime pie—this is a creamy coconut key lime pie made with a buttery cookie crust, fresh tart lime juice, condensed milk, and creamy coconut. I used both key lime and regular (aka persian) lime juice to test this pie, and in the end, they tasted very similar. Key limes are much harder to squeeze for juice but will offer a more fruity taste in the end. You'll need about 1 pound (455 g) key limes or 6 to 8 persian limes for the amount of juice used in this recipe.

PAY DE LIMÓN CON COCO
Coconut Key Lime Pie

Serves 6 to 8

FOR THE CRUST

1½ cups (139 g) Maria cookie (see Note on page 114) crumbs (from about 1 sleeve of Maria cookies)

3 tablespoons sugar

6 tablespoons (3 ounces/85 g) unsalted butter, melted

Pinch of salt

FOR THE FILLING

1 (14-ounce/397 g) can sweetened condensed milk

⅓ cup (103 g) cream of coconut (like Coco Lopez)

⅓ cup (80 g) sour cream

5 large egg yolks

Pinch of salt

⅔ cup (157 g) fresh key lime or regular lime juice

(continues)

+ Preheat the oven to 350°F (180°C). Lightly grease a 9-inch (23 cm) pie dish.

+ **Make the crust:** In a bowl, mix together the cookie crumbs and sugar. Add the melted butter and salt and mix to combine. Carefully press the crust into the pie dish so that there's an even layer on the bottom and up the sides, trying to make sure the bottom of the crust isn't too thin or the pie might have a hard time coming out in one piece.

+ Bake for 6 minutes, just enough to become fragrant and barely golden brown. Remove from the oven and set on a wire rack to cool while you make the filling. Leave the oven on.

+ **Make the filling:** In a large bowl, whisk together the condensed milk, cream of coconut, sour cream, egg yolks, and salt. The lime juice will create a reaction when combined with the condensed milk that will cause it to thicken, so the lime juice is not whisked in until right before you pour the filling into the crust.

+ Once the crust has cooled completely, whisk the lime juice into the bowl with the rest of the filling ingredients until everything is fully combined. Pour the filling into the crust. Return the dish to the oven and bake just until the filling is set and the center of the pie has a slight jiggle, about 15 minutes. The filling will finish setting in the refrigerator, so don't bake for any longer than 15 minutes to avoid overcooking.

+ Set the pie on a rack to cool to room temperature. Once cooled, place a piece of plastic wrap on the top to prevent a skin from forming and refrigerate for at least 4 hours. This helps the pie set further into a luscious tart consistency.

(continues)

FOR THE TOPPING

1 cup (227 g) heavy cream

3 tablespoons (56 g) cream of coconut

2 tablespoons (30 g) sour cream

TO FINISH

Grated lime zest (from 1 lime)

Toasted coconut chips

✦ **When you're ready to serve, make the topping:** In a stand mixer fitted with the whisk, beat the heavy cream, cream of coconut, and sour cream to a soft peak consistency. Pile the topping all over the pie (see Tip). The contrast of the whipped cream and tart pie is needed in every bite to be perfect, so there's no delicate piping job around the edge here.

✦ To finish, garnish the pie with lime zest and toasted coconut chips (save yourself the hassle and buy the already toasted ones at the store if available).

NOTE: Maria cookies are round buttery vanilla-flavored cookies that originated in England in the nineteenth century as Marie biscuits. They are now sold worldwide under many names, including in Mexico, where they are called galletas maria or just marias.

TIP: Because of the sour cream, the whipped topping is stabilized enough to not deflate in the refrigerator. If you want to make it an hour or two before serving, just place it on the pie and let it sit loosely covered in the refrigerator.

On birthdays, I could always count on my mom to make me a really good bowl of pozole blanco or birria, and for dessert she'd make a giant gelatina (jello) comprising a layer of creamy gelatina de leche and a layer of strawberry Jell-O and sliced fresh strawberries. It's a really simple dessert that you can modify to fit a Bundt pan. You can also make it in a glass baking dish for Jell-O squares, or in individual cups for a party.

STRAWBERRIES AND CREAM GELATINA

Serves 6 to 8

FOR THE STRAWBERRY LAYER

2 (6-ounce/170 g) packages strawberry-flavored gelatin

1½ cups (354 g) boiling water

1¾ cups (413 g) cold water plus 2 ice cubes

1 tablespoon fresh lime or lemon juice

3 cups (432 g) sliced hulled strawberries (from about 1 pound/455 g strawberries)

FOR THE CREAM LAYER

3 tablespoons unflavored gelatin

2 cups (472 g) whole milk

1½ teaspoons pure vanilla extract

1 (14-ounce/397 g) can sweetened condensed milk

6 ounces (170 g) full-fat cream cheese, at room temperature

+ Mist a 9 × 13-inch (23 × 33 cm) baking pan with cooking spray and set aside.

+ **Make the strawberry layer:** In a heatproof bowl, stir together the strawberry gelatin and boiling water until dissolved. Measure out 1¾ cups (413 g) cold water, then add 2 ice cubes. Add the ice water and lime juice to the hot strawberry gelatin mixture and stir until the ice has melted. The ice water speeds up the cooling and setting process of the gelatin so you don't have to wait as long to add the cream layer.

+ Pour the strawberry layer into the pan and top with the slices of strawberry, gently pushing them down if they're floating on top. Refrigerate for 1 hour to set.

+ **Make the cream layer:** Pour 1½ cups (354 g) water into a medium saucepan. Sprinkle the unflavored gelatin over the top and set this aside for 5 minutes to soften and bloom.

+ Meanwhile, in a blender, blend together the milk, vanilla, condensed milk, and cream cheese until smooth with no chunks of cream cheese remaining, about 30 seconds. Pour into a large bowl and set aside.

+ Place the saucepan with the softened gelatin over medium-low heat and cook, stirring occasionally, just until the gelatin has dissolved. Once the gelatin has dissolved, stir it into the cream cheese base until thoroughly mixed.

+ Pour the cream layer over the strawberry layer and return to the refrigerator for another hour before serving.

+ To serve, you can either flip it out onto a serving platter so the strawberry layer is on top or serve it straight from the pan. Store in the refrigerator covered with plastic wrap for up to 2 days. If you store the dessert any longer than that, the fruit starts to turn mealy.

Since I like to use half-and-half in my flans, turning a warm cup of café con leche into a flan was a no-brainer. I like to steep crushed coffee beans in half-and-half to extract and infuse their flavor into the custard without having to water it down. The result is a rich and creamy cup of coffee in the form of a classic flan.

CAFÉ CON LECHE FLAN

Serves 8 to 10

FOR THE COFFEE CREAM
1¾ cups (413 g) half-and-half

¼ cup (20 g) medium-roast coffee beans, roughly crushed

FOR THE CARAMEL
1 cup (200 g) granulated sugar

FOR THE FLAN
3 large eggs

1 (14-ounce/397 g) can sweetened condensed milk

2 teaspoons pure vanilla extract

Pinch of salt

✦ **Make the coffee cream:** In a small saucepan, stir together the half-and-half and coffee beans and cook over low heat for 30 minutes, stirring occasionally so the bottom doesn't burn. Let cool completely, then strain the coffee cream into a measuring cup.

✦ Preheat the oven to 300°F (150°C). Mist an 8-inch (20 cm) cake pan with cooking spray.

✦ **Make the caramel:** In a medium saucepan, combine the sugar and ¼ cup (59 g) water over low heat. Increase the heat to medium and cook, occasionally swirling the pan to distribute the caramelized sugar (but do not stir the sugar or it will seize and crystallize), until the mixture turns amber in color, 8 to 12 minutes. As soon as all the sugar has turned an amber color, quickly and carefully pour the caramel into the prepared cake pan. Let this cool for 5 minutes.

✦ **Make the flan:** In a blender, combine the coffee cream, eggs, condensed milk, vanilla, and salt and blend until smooth, 20 to 30 seconds.

✦ Place the cake pan in a larger shallow metal baking dish like a roasting pan. Pour the custard into the cake pan and cover the cake pan tightly with foil. Fill the larger baking dish with warm or hot water to come halfway up the side of the cake pan.

✦ Bake until the outer rim of the custard is firm but the center still has some jiggle to it, 1 hour 15 minutes to 1 hour 30 minutes. Remove the cake pan from the water bath, pull off the foil and set aside, and let cool at room temperature for about 1 hour. Place the foil back onto the cake pan and refrigerate for at least 4 hours until well chilled and completely set.

✦ When you're ready to serve, run a thin sharp knife around the edge of the cake pan to make sure the flan doesn't stick, then place a plate on top and quickly flip it over to invert. Lift off the cake pan and serve.

Presentation is the key to making even the simplest of pastries look expensive, and these pinwheels are no exception! Just a simple fold in the puff pastry makes these pastries with a vanilla bean cream cheese filling and a dollop of dulce de leche look as though they took great skill to create. (But it'll be our little secret.)

CREAM CHEESE AND DULCE DE LECHE PINWHEELS

Makes 12 pastries

12 ounces (340 g) full-fat cream cheese, at room temperature

½ cup (100 g) sugar

1½ teaspoons vanilla bean paste

Pinch of salt

2 (225 g) sheets frozen puff pastry, thawed but still cold (see Tip)

Generous ¾ cup (170 g) dulce de leche

FOR THE EGG WASH
1 large egg, whisked

FOR THE CINNAMON SUGAR
2 tablespoons sugar
½ teaspoon ground cinnamon

✦ In a stand mixer fitted with the paddle, combine the cream cheese, sugar, vanilla bean paste, and salt. Beat for 30 seconds on medium speed, then scrape down the sides of the bowl and beat on medium speed for a full minute.

✦ Line two baking sheets with parchment paper. Cut the puff pastry along each of the creases (from where the pastry was folded to fit into the packaging) to make 3 rectangles. Then cut each of those in half crosswise to create 6 equal rectangles. Use a rolling pin to gently roll each rectangle into a 6-inch (15 cm) square, then transfer to one of the lined baking sheets, making sure you space all six square pieces of puff pastry evenly. Repeat with the remaining puff pastry sheet and second baking sheet.

✦ Brush about a 1-inch (2.5 cm) border around the edge of each square with some egg wash. Use a knife to cut a 2½-inch (6.5 cm) slit from each corner toward the center. Fold every other corner toward the center to form the pinwheel, then use a finger to press the corners together in the center to secure. Brush these folds with the egg wash, then lightly sprinkle each pinwheel arm with the cinnamon sugar.

✦ Add 2 tablespoons of the cream cheese filling to the center of each pinwheel, then use a spoon to make a small well inside the cream cheese, and spoon or pipe 1 tablespoon (19 g) dulce de leche into the center.

✦ Refrigerate the baking sheets for 30 minutes to chill.

✦ Preheat the oven to 400°F (200°C).

✦ Bake the pinwheels until they are puffed and golden, 16 to 18 minutes. Let cool for 10 minutes before serving.

TIP: To thaw the puff pastry, I unfold the sheets and place them on a baking sheet lined with parchment paper at room temperature for 1 hour. But make sure the puff pastry is still cold. If you let the sheets thaw completely, they will be soft and flimsy, and will be harder to work with.

I love oatmeal cookies. I'm sorry, but I do! Raisins might turn people off the classic oatmeal cookie, so in my version, I decided to toss out the raisins and swap in dried sweetened hibiscus for a lightly sweet but tart punch. Hibiscus is the same flower you use to make tea or agua fresca, but in this case the flowers have been sweetened and dried and are intended to be eaten the way you would eat dried fruit. White chocolate balances out their tart kiss while also playing well with the toasted oats in the cookie. If you are having problems finding dried sweetened hibiscus locally, you can purchase it online. If you still cannot find it but want to try these cookies, you can always substitute an equal amount of a dried sweetened fruit such as cranberries or cherries.

HIBISCUS AND WHITE CHOCOLATE OATMEAL COOKIES

Makes 18 cookies

⅔ cup (83 g) all-purpose flour

¾ teaspoon baking soda

½ teaspoon ground Ceylon or Mexican cinnamon

¼ teaspoon Diamond Crystal kosher salt or ⅛ teaspoon fine sea salt

½ cup (8 tablespoons/115 g) unsalted butter

⅓ cup (69 g) light brown sugar

⅓ cup (67 g) granulated sugar

1 teaspoon pure vanilla extract

1 large egg

1½ cups (150 g) old-fashioned rolled oats

¾ cup (60 g) finely chopped dried sweetened hibiscus

½ cup (73 g) white chocolate chips (or any other chocolate chip, such as semisweet or milk chocolate)

✦ In a large bowl, mix together the flour, baking soda, cinnamon, and salt. Set aside.

✦ In a stand mixer fitted with the paddle, cream together the butter, both sugars, and the vanilla until light and fluffy, about 1 minute. Add the egg and mix until combined. Scrape down the sides of the bowl with a silicone spatula and add the flour mixture. Mix on medium speed just until combined. Add the oats, hibiscus, and chocolate chips and mix for about 15 seconds longer. Scrape down the sides to make sure no batter is left behind and mix once more for a few seconds.

✦ Line a large baking sheet with parchment paper. Using a spoon or medium cookie scoop, scoop out 1½-tablespoon portions of the dough onto the lined baking sheet (no need to shape them). Cover lightly with plastic wrap and refrigerate for at least 30 minutes to chill. This will help the oats hydrate a little more and give a thicker, chewier cookie in the end. You can also freeze them to bake later (see Tip).

✦ When you're ready to bake, preheat the oven to 350°F (180°C). Line another baking sheet with parchment paper.

✦ Roll the scoops of dough into smooth round balls and place on the two baking sheets 1½ inches (4 cm) apart. You should be able to fit about 9 cookies on a sheet.

(continues)

✦ One sheet at a time, bake the cookies until the edges and the tops are just barely golden brown and the middles still look a little underbaked, 12 to 14 minutes. Let the cookies cool on the pan for 5 minutes, then transfer them to a rack to cool completely.

✦ Store the cookies in a sealed container for up to 3 days at room temperature.

TIP: To freeze cookie dough, refrigerate the balls of dough for a couple of hours, then transfer them to a zip-top freezer bag. Freeze the balls in a single layer so they don't stick together. Frozen cookie dough can be baked straight from the freezer and doesn't need to thaw. Simply add an extra minute or two of baking time!

When I was in high school, I often spent my weekends having to wake up early to go off to work with my dad in construction. Those weekends were tough, but they helped shape my work ethic, and gave my dad and me a chance to bond over donuts before we'd get to a job. In Santa Ana, where I grew up, there's a donut shop off Bristol Street called Christy's Donuts, where they came to recognize us as regulars. My donut of choice was always the cream cheese danish with strawberry jam. These danishes are super simple to make because they use store-bought puff pastry and have a vanilla bean cream cheese filling that also includes my own version of their berry filling made with blueberries, blackberries, and raspberries, and tropical hibiscus. This recipe calls for a total of 8 ounces (227 g) berries so feel free to use a mix of whatever berries are in season—just make sure it totals 8 ounces.

BERRY HIBISCUS DANISHES

Makes 12

FOR THE PASTRY

2 (225 g) sheets frozen puff pastry

FOR THE BERRY-HIBISCUS SAUCE

¼ cup (12 g) dried hibiscus flowers

½ cup (118 g) boiling water

3 ounces (85g) mixed ripe berries (I like to use blueberries, blackberries, and raspberries)

¼ cup (50 g) sugar

1½ teaspoons lime juice

1½ teaspoons cornstarch

FOR THE CREAM CHEESE FILLING

1 pound (455 g) full-fat cream cheese, at room temperature

⅔ cup (134 g) sugar

1 large egg yolk

1 tablespoon lime juice

2½ teaspoons vanilla bean paste

½ teaspoon Diamond Crystal kosher salt or ¼ teaspoon fine sea salt

(continues)

✦ Thaw the puff pastry (see Tip on page 127).

✦ **Meanwhile, make the berry–hibiscus sauce:** In a small heatproof bowl, combine the hibiscus and boiling water and set aside to let steep for 20 minutes.

✦ Once the hibiscus is done steeping, strain the hibiscus tea into a blender, then add the berries and blend for 30 to 45 seconds, until smooth.

✦ Pour the berry puree into a small saucepan, then stir in the sugar, lime juice, and cornstarch and set over medium heat. Cook the mixture until it starts to bubble and thicken, stirring occasionally. Once it starts to bubble, cook for a full minute to make sure the cornstarch is fully activated. Remove the sauce from the flame and set aside to cool.

✦ **Make the cream cheese filling:** In a stand mixer fitted with the paddle, combine the cream cheese, sugar, egg yolk, lime juice, vanilla bean paste, and salt. Beat for 30 seconds on medium speed, then scrape down the sides of the bowl and beat on medium speed for a full minute.

✦ Line two large baking sheets with parchment paper.

✦ Once the puff pastry sheets have thawed, cut along each of the creases (from where the pastry was folded to fit into the packaging). Cut once more down the middle crosswise to create 6 equal-size rectangles. Use a rolling pin to gently roll each piece of dough into a 3½ × 4½-inch (9 × 10 cm) rectangle. Evenly space 6 rectangles of puff pastry per baking sheet. Repeat with the remaining puff pastry sheet until you have a total of 12 rectangles.

(continues)

FOR THE EGG WASH

**1 large egg whisked with
1 tablespoon cold water**

TO ASSEMBLE

**5 ounces (142g) mixed ripe
berries**

✦ Use a fork to gently prick the surface of each piece of puff pastry all over, then brush the outer edges of each with the egg wash. Spoon or pipe 3 to 3½ tablespoons of the cream cheese filling in the center. Refrigerate the pastries for at least 30 minutes to chill.

✦ Meanwhile, preheat the oven to 400°F (200°C).

✦ Bake the danishes until puffed and golden, 16 to 18 minutes. Let cool for 10 minutes before serving. Once you are ready to serve, drizzle about 1 tablespoon of the berry sauce over the cream cheese filling, then top with a couple of berries.

TIP: To thaw the puff pastry, unfold the sheets and place on a baking sheet lined with parchment paper. Thaw at room temperature for about 1 hour, but not longer than that because you want the pastry to still be cold but easy to work with. If pastry thaws too much, it'll be very soft and flimsy.

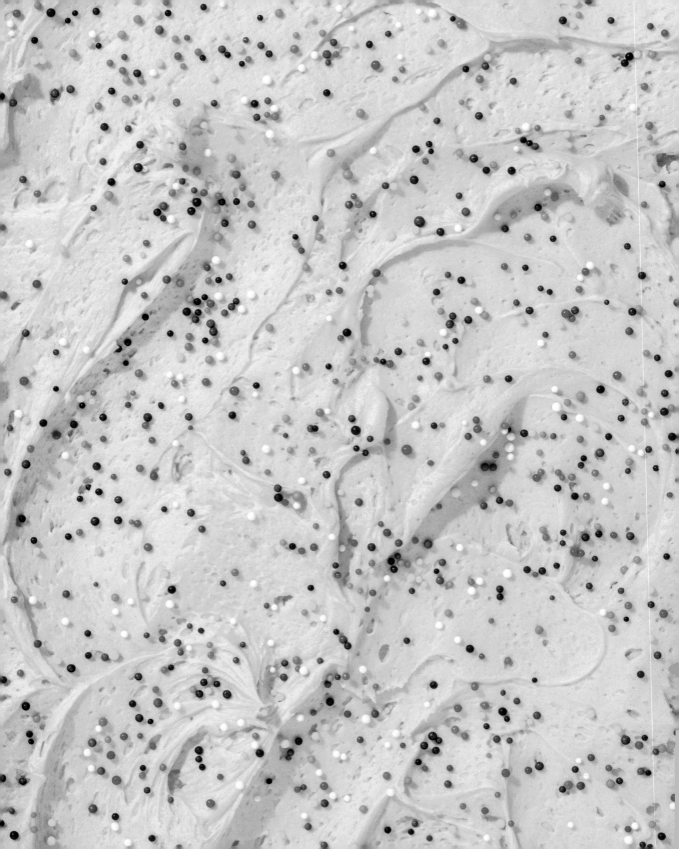

PASTELES

The centerpiece of every party is the cake, and with my dulce de leche choco-flan being one of the shining stars from *Chicano Eats*, I knew I had to create an entire chapter to celebrate a good slice. You're going to find not one but *three* new recipes for chocoflan: a caramel chocoflan, a red velvet choco-flan (which features cream cheese flan and moist red velvet cake layers), and a pumpkin chocoflan that tastes just like fall.

Boxed cake mix is what initially got me into baking when I was a senior in high school. I'd run across the street to get myself strawberry cake mix and a little tub of frosting. Somehow, even with my lack of tools and knowl-edge, everything always came together. Being able to engineer a red velvet chocoflan (from scratch) makes me happy to see how far I've come along.

I'm especially excited for you to make my horchata sheet cake, which features a horchata buttercream that uses the ermine frosting (or boiled milk frosting) technique. It's one of my favorite ways to amplify subtle flavors in a buttercream! I have plenty of options for all seasons, but if you need a place to start, my classic tres leches is always a good choice; it tastes just like a birthday party from my childhood!

CAKES

Chocoflan has been referred to as the "impossible" cake because when you make it, you first add the cake batter to the pan and then pour in the flan—and during the baking process they switch places. Chocoflan is basically a magic trick you can eat! When you invert the cake out of the pan you end up with a bottom layer of moist chocolate cake and a classic vanilla flan on top.

CLASSIC CHOCOFLAN

Serves 16

FOR THE PAN
⅓ cup (100 g) dulce de leche
   or cajeta

FOR THE FLAN
1 (14-ounce/397 g) can
   sweetened condensed milk

1 (12-ounce/340g) can
   evaporated milk

4 ounces (115 g) full-fat cream
   cheese, at room temperature

1½ teaspoons pure vanilla extract

Pinch of salt

5 large eggs

FOR THE CHOCOLATE CAKE
1⅓ cups (167 g) unbleached
   all-purpose flour

1 cup (200 g) sugar

½ cup (45 g) unsweetened
   cocoa powder

1 teaspoon baking soda

½ teaspoon baking powder

½ teaspoon Diamond Crystal
   kosher salt or ¼ teaspoon
   fine sea salt

½ teaspoon ground cinnamon

(continues)

✦ Preheat the oven to 350°F (180°C).

✦ **Prepare the pan:** Liberally coat a 10-cup Bundt pan (see Note on page 144)with cooking spray. Drizzle the dulce de leche into the bottom of the pan.

✦ **Make the flan custard:** In a blender, combine the condensed milk, evaporated milk, cream cheese, vanilla, and salt and blend until smooth, 20 to 30 seconds. Add the eggs and blend for another 10 seconds until smooth.

✦ **Make the chocolate cake batter:** Sift the flour, sugar, cocoa powder, baking soda, baking powder, salt, and cinnamon directly into the bowl of a stand mixer fitted with the paddle. Mix on the lowest setting until just combined. Add the softened butter and continue mixing on low speed until the mixture resembles wet sand. Stop the mixer and scrape down the sides of the bowl if needed.

✦ In a spouted measuring cup, combine the coffee, buttermilk, egg, and vanilla and whisk to combine. With the mixer running on low speed, slowly pour the liquid mixture into the flour/butter mixture. Scrape down the sides of the bowl and beat the mixture on high for a full minute.

✦ **Assemble the chocoflan:** Pour the cake batter into the prepared Bundt pan, smoothing out the top with an offset spatula or spoon. Carefully ladle in the flan so you disturb the cake batter as little as possible. Transfer the Bundt pan to a roasting pan or baking dish large enough to fit the Bundt pan. Grease a piece of foil and place it greased side down onto the Bundt pan, folding it over the edges to loosely seal it.

✦ Transfer the roasting pan with the Bundt pan to a pulled-out oven rack. Pour water (from the tap is fine) into the roasting pan or baking dish to come 2 to 3 inches (5 to 7.5 cm) up the sides of the Bundt pan.

✦ Bake until a skewer inserted into the cake comes out with little to no crumbs sticking to it, 1 hour 30 minutes to 1 hour 45 minutes. Start checking for doneness at the 1½-hour mark.

(continues)

6 tablespoons (85 g) unsalted butter, cubed, at room temperature

½ cup (120 g) brewed coffee

½ cup (114 g) buttermilk

1 large egg

1 teaspoon pure vanilla extract

FOR SERVING

Dulce de leche and chopped nuts, or whipped cream and ground cinnamon

✦ Carefully remove the Bundt pan from the roasting pan and let it cool to room temperature before placing it in the refrigerator to cool completely, for at least a couple of hours.

✦ Once you're ready to serve, carefully run a knife around any edges that are still sticking, then invert onto a serving platter, gently shaking it up and down if it's being difficult (if it was greased properly, you shouldn't have any major issues). I like to dip the bottom of the Bundt pan in a bowl of hot water for 2 to 3 minutes and then invert it to make sure it doesn't stick.

✦ If desired, serve with dulce de leche and a sprinkle of chopped nuts or with whipped cream and a sprinkle of cinnamon.

This cheesecake consists of a crust made from canelitas—a beloved Mexican cinnamon sugar cookie I enjoyed as a kid—with a cinnamon and brown sugar/cream cheese filling. To top things off, we're layering this cheesecake with a brown sugar/cinnamon swirl that makes it look like you've got some serious skill. If you have any extra time, make a batch of homemade whipped cream to top the cheesecake. If you have any extra canelitas, crumble them over the whipped cream or simply sprinkle a little bit of cinnamon over the cake and finish it off with a drizzle of cajeta.

CHURRO CHEESECAKE

Makes one 9-inch (23 cm) cheesecake

FOR THE CRUST

9 ounces (255 g) Marinela Canelitas (24 cookies); (see Note on page 135)

¼ teaspoon Diamond Crystal kosher salt or ⅛ teaspoon fine sea salt

⅓ cup (76 g) unsalted butter, melted

FOR THE CHEESECAKE FILLING

24 ounces (680 g) full-fat cream cheese, at room temperature

¼ cup (52 g) sour cream

1 teaspoon pure vanilla extract

1 cup (208 g) light brown sugar

1¼ teaspoons ground cinnamon

¼ teaspoon Diamond Crystal kosher salt or ⅛ teaspoon fine sea salt

2 large eggs, at room temperature

(continues)

✦ **Make the crust:** In a food processor or blender, pulse the canelita cookies until the mixture resembles fine sand, 45 seconds to 1 minute. Pour the cookie mixture into a large bowl, sprinkle in the salt, then pour in the melted butter. Use your hands or a rubber spatula to make sure the melted butter is evenly distributed. Set aside.

✦ Wrap the outside of a 9-inch (23 cm) springform pan with foil (to keep water from seeping in). Lightly coat the inside with cooking spray. Pour in the crust mixture, evenly distribute, and use the bottom of a measuring cup to press it into the bottom of the pan and about 1 inch (2.5 cm) up the sides of the pan. Set the springform inside a roasting pan or bigger shallow baking pan. Set aside.

✦ **Make the cheesecake filling:** In a stand mixer fitted with the paddle, beat the cream cheese on low speed, slowly increasing to medium speed, until smooth, 30 to 45 seconds. Reduce the speed to low and beat in the sour cream, then the vanilla until well incorporated. Add the brown sugar, cinnamon, and salt and beat together for a minute. Add the eggs, one at a time, beating just to incorporate after each addition. Turn the mixer off to make sure you don't incorporate too much air (which makes the cheesecake inflate and crack), then use a silicone spatula to scrape down the sides of the bowl. Turn the mixer back on low and let it run for 15 seconds, just to make sure everything is fully incorporated, then set the cheesecake mixture aside.

✦ **Make the brown sugar/cinnamon swirl:** In a large bowl, whisk together the brown sugar, cinnamon, and cornstarch. Whisk in 1 tablespoon cold water until the slurry comes together.

✦ Preheat the oven to 350°F (180°C).

✦ Pour the cheesecake filling into the springform pan, then use an offset spatula to make sure the batter is evenly distributed. Use a spoon to drizzle the brown sugar swirl over the cheesecake batter, then use a toothpick and insert it about ¼ inch (.63 cm) into the batter and move it around in circles to create swirls.

(continues)

**FOR THE BROWN SUGAR/
CINNAMON SWIRL**

¼ cup (52 g) light brown sugar

1 teaspoon ground cinnamon

1½ teaspoons cornstarch

FOR SERVING

Whipped cream

Ground cinnamon

Cajeta or dulce de leche

✦ Place the roasting pan on a pulled-out rack of the oven and fill the pan with water to come halfway up the sides of the springform. Bake until the outer edges are firm, but the center still has a slight jiggle to it, about 1 hour 10 minutes.

✦ Turn the oven off, slightly crack open the oven door, and leave the cheesecake inside the oven to rest for 1 hour. This will ensure that it doesn't crack. Cracks tend to form when the cheesecake cools too quickly.

✦ Remove the cheesecake from the oven and set it on the counter to cool completely, 2 to 3 hours. If it doesn't cool thoroughly, the cheesecake will form condensation while it's refrigerated.

✦ Cover with plastic wrap and refrigerate for at least 6 hours, but preferably overnight to set.

✦ Gently remove the foil from the sides of the springform pan and use a 10- to 12-inch (25 to 30 cm) offset spatula (or a long thin knife) to run it around the perimeter of the cheesecake to loosen it from the base of the pan and push it onto a cake stand.

✦ To serve, cut the cheesecake into wedges, cleaning the knife blade after each cut for a cleaner slice. Garnish with a dollop of freshly whipped cream, a sprinkle of cinnamon, and a drizzle of cajeta or dulce de leche.

NOTE: If you can't find the canelitas, use 2 cups (240 g) graham cracker crumbs, 1 tablespoon sugar, and 1 teaspoon ground cinnamon. Combine with the salt and melted butter as directed to make the crust.

When I was kid, tres leches was always the cake of choice for celebrations. It was never my favorite because the topping always tasted bitter from the food coloring used to decorate the cake. As an adult, I've developed a recipe for my own version that keeps all of the good. This cake has a light vanilla whipped topping, and if you happen to have any Frangelico (hazelnut liqueur) on hand, add a tablespoon as it whips and thank me later!

TRES LECHES

Serves 12 to 16

FOR THE CAKE

2 cups (250 g) unbleached all-purpose flour

1½ teaspoons baking powder

1 teaspoon baking soda

1 teaspoon Diamond Crystal kosher salt or ½ teaspoon fine sea salt

1 cup (229 g) buttermilk

4 large eggs

1 teaspoon pure vanilla extract

½ cup (8 tablespoons/115 g) unsalted butter, at room temperature

1 cup (200 g) granulated sugar

FOR THE TRES LECHES

1 (14-ounce/397 g) can sweetened condensed milk

1 (12-ounce/340 g) can evaporated milk

2 cups (472 g) whole milk

1 teaspoon pure vanilla extract

¼ teaspoon Diamond Crystal kosher salt or ⅛ teaspoon fine sea salt

(continues)

✦ **Make the cake:** Preheat the oven to 350°F (180°C). Mist a 9 × 13-inch (23 × 33 cm) pan with cooking spray.

✦ In a large bowl, whisk together the flour, baking powder, baking soda, and salt. In a large spouted cup, whisk together the buttermilk, eggs, and vanilla. Set both aside.

✦ In a stand mixer fitted with the paddle, cream the butter and granulated sugar on medium speed for 2½ minutes, until the mixture is fluffy and pale in color. Reduce the speed to medium-low, then pour in one-third of the buttermilk mixture followed by one-third of the flour mixture. Repeat this process until all of the flour mixture and buttermilk have been incorporated.

✦ Pour the cake batter into the greased pan and use an offset spatula to evenly distribute the batter. Bake until the top is golden brown and a toothpick inserted into the middle of the cake comes out clean, 22 to 25 minutes. Let the cake cool completely in the pan.

✦ **Meanwhile, make the tres leches:** In a large bowl with a spout, whisk together the condensed milk, evaporated milk, whole milk, vanilla, and salt.

✦ After the cake has cooled completely, use a toothpick to poke holes in it, then pour the milk mixture on top. Cover the cake with plastic wrap, then refrigerate for at least 2 hours.

(continues)

FOR THE WHIPPED TOPPING

1⅓ cups (303 g) heavy cream

⅓ cup (69 g) sour cream

⅓ cup (33 g) powdered sugar, sifted

1 teaspoon pure vanilla extract (or substitute with vanilla bean paste)

1½ tablespoons hazelnut liqueur (optional)

FOR THE GARNISH

2 cups (288 g) fresh berries (use a mix of your favorites)

✦ **Make the whipped topping:** In a stand mixer fitted with the whisk, beat the heavy cream, sour cream, powdered sugar, and vanilla on low speed until combined. Bump up the speed to medium-high and beat for about 2 minutes for medium peaks, and about 3 minutes for firm peaks. I prefer medium peaks.

✦ Use an offset spatula to spread the whipped topping evenly over the cake, then garnish with fresh berries.

This is one of my favorite cake recipes—it tastes just like horchata! This cake features an ermine (boiled milk) frosting, which means the buttercream has a base consisting of a sweet pudding made up of horchata and sugar, with flour to thicken it. I love using this technique for the buttercream base because it amplifies the horchata flavor even more. Be sure to use a milky horchata, as it makes for a creamier buttercream and better flavor in the end.

HORCHATA SHEET CAKE

Serves 12 to 16

FOR THE CAKE

2½ cups (312 g) unbleached all-purpose flour

2½ teaspoons baking powder

1 teaspoon ground cinnamon

½ teaspoon Diamond Crystal kosher salt or ¼ teaspoon fine sea salt

¾ cup (12 tablespoons/170 g) unsalted butter, at room temperature

1¾ cups (350 g) sugar

2 teaspoons pure vanilla extract

3 large eggs

1⅓ cups (305 g) buttermilk

FOR THE BUTTERCREAM

6 tablespoons (47 g) unbleached all-purpose flour

1½ cups (300 g) sugar

¼ teaspoon Diamond Crystal kosher salt or ⅛ teaspoon fine sea salt

1½ cups (354 g) horchata (from your favorite taquería)

(continues)

✦ **Make the cake:** Preheat the oven to 350°F (180°C). Lightly grease a 9 × 13-inch (23 × 33 cm) cake pan.

✦ In a medium bowl, whisk together the flour, baking powder, cinnamon, and salt and set aside.

✦ In a stand mixer fitted with the paddle, beat the butter with the sugar on medium speed for 2½ minutes, until light and fluffy and paler in color. Add the vanilla and eggs, one at a time, beating well after each addition. Add one-third of the dry ingredients, mix on low to incorporate, then one-third of the buttermilk, followed by another third of the dry mixture, another third of the buttermilk, and then finally the last amount of each. Mix just until combined, then use a silicone spatula to scrape down the sides of the bowl to make sure everything's mixed in.

✦ Scrape the batter into the prepared pan, smooth it out, and bake until the cake is lightly golden brown and a toothpick or skewer inserted into the center of the cake comes out clean, 30 to 35 minutes. Let the cake cool completely in the pan.

✦ **Make the buttercream:** In a small saucepan, combine the flour, sugar, and salt. Whisk in the horchata until everything has been fully incorporated. Set over medium-low heat and bring the mixture to a boil, whisking occasionally to make sure it doesn't burn. Once it reaches a boil, reduce the heat and continue whisking until the pudding has thickened, about 2 minutes. Use a silicone spatula to transfer the pudding to a plate and immediately press plastic wrap onto the surface to prevent a skin from forming. Let it cool for a few minutes, then refrigerate for about 1 hour or until it has cooled completely.

(continues)

1½ cups (342 g) unsalted butter, at room temperature

1 teaspoon vanilla bean paste

1½ teaspoons ground cinnamon

FOR THE HORCHATA SOAK

⅔ cup (157 g) horchata (from your favorite taquería)

FOR THE GARNISH

1 tablespoon ground cinnamon

✦ In a stand mixer fitted with the whisk, beat the butter on medium speed with the vanilla and cinnamon for a minute. With the mixer on low, add the cooled pudding mixture 1 tablespoon at a time until it's all been added to the bowl, then boost the speed to medium-high and beat until the frosting is light and fluffy, 2 to 3 minutes.

✦ **Soak the cake:** Use a toothpick to poke small holes on the surface of the cake, then drizzle the horchata over the cake to soak. Spread the frosting evenly over the cake. Return the cake to the refrigerator for 30 to 45 minutes to firm up the frosting. (This makes for a clean cut, and to me, cold buttercream just tastes so much better!) Garnish the cake with an even sprinkle of ground cinnamon.

I wasn't sure how I was going to top the dulce de leche chocoflan from my first cookbook that was so popular—then it hit me: red velvet chocoflan! This chocoflan consists of a moist red velvet cake layer, and tangy cream cheese flan.

RED VELVET CHOCOFLAN

Serves 16

FOR THE FLAN

1 (14-ounce/397 g) can sweetened condensed milk

1½ cups (354 g) half-and-half

8 ounces (227 g) full-fat cream cheese, at room temperature

½ teaspoon pure vanilla extract

Pinch of salt

4 large eggs

FOR THE RED VELVET CAKE

1½ cups (188 g) unbleached all-purpose flour

1 cup (200 g) sugar

¼ cup (22 g) unsweetened cocoa powder

1 teaspoon baking soda

½ teaspoon baking powder

½ teaspoon Diamond Crystal kosher salt or ¼ teaspoon fine sea salt

½ cup (8 tablespoons/115 g) unsalted butter, cubed, at room temperature

1 cup (229 g) buttermilk, at room temperature

1 large egg, at room temperature

2 tablespoons neutral oil, like canola or avocado

1 teaspoon pure vanilla extract

1 teaspoon red gel food coloring

✦ Preheat the oven to 350°F (180°C). Mist a 10-cup Bundt pan (see Note on page 144) well with cooking spray. Cut out a square of foil large enough to cover the top of the Bundt pan and mist it, too.

✦ **Make the flan:** In a blender, combine the condensed milk, half-and-half, cream cheese, vanilla, and salt. Blend for 1 minute on medium-high speed, then add the eggs and blend on medium-high for just about 10 seconds. Try not to blend for too long after you add the eggs so you don't whip too much air into the flan. Set this mixture aside.

✦ **Make the red velvet cake:** In a stand mixer fitted with the paddle, combine the flour, sugar, cocoa powder, baking soda, baking powder, and salt. Add the cubed butter to the dry ingredients and mix on low until the mixture looks like wet sand.

✦ Pour the buttermilk into a large spouted cup, add the egg, oil, vanilla, and food coloring and mix to combine. With the mixer on low, slowly pour in the wet ingredients, then once all the liquid has been added, stop the mixer and scrape down the sides of the bowl. Turn the mixer to medium and let it run for a full minute to make sure everything is fully incorporated.

✦ Pour the cake batter into the prepared Bundt pan. Gently pour the flan over the top of the cake batter by pouring it into a ladle and letting it flow over the edge. This allows the flan to be added without disturbing the cake batter that much. (This is the opposite of how the finished chocoflan looks. The two batters will swap places in the oven.) Light marbling is normal, and depending on the dye you use it might be more apparent as the batters swap places while baking, but if you aren't gentle when pouring in the flan mixture, you'll have chunks of cake baking into the flan.

✦ Place the square of foil greased side down onto the Bundt pan and wrap it around the outside edge of the pan. No need to wrap it super tightly, but try not to just leave it sitting on top. Place the Bundt pan in a large roasting pan. Place the roasting pan on a pulled-out rack of the oven. Fill the roasting pan roughly two-thirds of the way up the sides with warm water (a large pitcher with a good spout is your best friend here) and close the oven door.

(continues)

✦ Bake until a short bamboo skewer or cake tester comes out with only a few crumbs from the cake, 1 hour 45 minutes to 2 hours. Start checking on it at the 1 hour 45-minute mark and note that if the skewer goes into the flan its tip might be a little wet because the flan won't have set yet; it will do that in the refrigerator.

✦ Carefully remove the roasting pan from the oven and carefully lift the Bundt pan out of the water bath and place it on a cooling rack. Let the chocoflan cool completely at room temperature with the foil tented on top of the pan, which will take about 2 hours.

✦ Place the foil tightly back onto the pan and place the chocoflan in the refrigerator to set completely. This should take 4 to 5 hours, but an overnight 6- to 8-hour chill is ideal for the flan to set up perfectly.

✦ When you're ready to serve, carefully use the tips of your fingers to pull the cake away from the edge of the pan, then place a large serving platter or cake stand over the Bundt pan and flip both over to invert. Depending on your pan the chocoflan might be a little difficult to invert at first. If this is the case, dip the bottom of the pan into a bowl of warm water for 5 to 6 minutes before trying to invert the cake again.

✦ To store, carefully wrap it in plastic wrap and keep in the refrigerator for up to 3 days.

NOTE: I developed all of the chocoflan recipes using a basic Wilton Bundt pan and I noticed that when I used pans with more intricate designs, the baking time increased by 10 to 15 minutes, and that caused too much marbling. The simpler the Bundt pan, the easier it will be for the batters to swap places during the baking process.

If I'm baking a cake for myself, it's going to be this one. Celebrations at my house usually consist of my husband and me and our three dogs, Nomi, Rigby, and Jepsen, so I like to keep things pretty simple and no fuss. This cake is exactly that and tastes like nostalgia, with a moist buttermilk yellow cake and a buttercream that's made with a Mexican chocolate ganache that makes each bite taste just like chocolate caliente (hot chocolate)!

CHICANO EATS BIRTHDAY CAKE

Serves 12 to 16

FOR THE CAKE

2½ cups (312 g) unbleached all-purpose flour

2½ teaspoons baking powder

½ teaspoon Diamond Crystal kosher salt or ¼ teaspoon fine sea salt

¾ cup (12 tablespoons/170 g) unsalted butter, at room temperature

1¾ cups (350 g) granulated sugar

1½ teaspoons vanilla extract

3 large eggs

1⅓ cups (305 g) buttermilk

FOR THE BUTTERCREAM

⅔ cup (151 g) heavy cream

⅔ cup (3½ ounces/100 g) grated Mexican chocolate

¾ cup (66 g) unsweetened cocoa powder

½ teaspoon Diamond Crystal kosher salt or ¼ teaspoon fine sea salt

(continues)

✦ **Make the cake:** Preheat the oven to 350°F (180°C). Grease two 8-inch (20 cm) round cake pans and line them with parchment paper rounds.

✦ In a medium bowl, whisk together the flour, baking powder, and salt. Set aside.

✦ In a stand mixer fitted with the paddle, beat the butter with the sugar on medium speed until light and fluffy and paler in color, about 2 minutes. Add the vanilla and eggs, one at a time, beating well after each addition. Add one-third of the dry ingredients, and mix on low to incorporate. Then add one-third of the buttermilk, followed by another third of the dry mixture, another third of the buttermilk, and then finally the last amount of each. Mix just until combined, then use a silicone spatula to scrape down the sides of the bowl to make sure everything's mixed in.

✦ Divide the batter evenly between the pans, smooth it out, and bake until the cake is lightly golden brown and a toothpick or skewer inserted into the center of the cake comes out clean, 34 to 36 minutes. Let the cakes cool completely in the pan.

✦ **Make the buttercream:** In a small saucepan, heat the cream over medium heat to just below a simmer. Remove from the heat and add the Mexican chocolate. Whisk until the chocolate has dissolved, then sift in the cocoa powder and salt. Whisk quickly once the cocoa has been incorporated to get rid of any lumps. Transfer the chocolate base to a bowl and press plastic wrap directly on the surface of the mixture. Set aside to cool completely to room temperature.

(continues)

1 cup (16 tablespoons/227 g) unsalted butter, at room temperature

3 cups (300 g) powdered sugar, sifted

1½ teaspoons pure vanilla extract

FOR SERVING
Rainbow sprinkles

✦ In a stand mixer fitted with the paddle, beat the butter on medium-high speed for 1 full minute. Add the powdered sugar ½ cup (50 g) at a time. Once all of the sugar has been added, beat for another full minute, then scrape down the sides of the bowl and add the vanilla extract and the cooled chocolate base. Beat on high for a final full minute, then scrape down the sides of the bowl and mix to finish incorporating any streaks of the butter mixture.

✦ Get the cake layers out of the pans, then add a heaping cup (185 g) of buttercream to the top of the bottom cake layer and use an offset spatula to smooth it out. Place the second cake layer on top and use an offset spatula to evenly spread a thin layer of buttercream (the "crumb coat") all over the top and sides of the cake, filling in the gaps where the layers meet with frosting to make the outside of the cake smooth. Refrigerate for 45 minutes to firm up the crumb coat.

✦ Beat the remaining buttercream on medium speed for about a minute, then finish frosting the cake. Once the cake is frosted, store it in the refrigerator until ready to serve. Garnish with rainbow sprinkles.

Okay, hear me out. This fancy-sounding "carlota de mango con limón" is actually just an icebox cake—and it's perfect for those hot days when turning on the oven to make something sweet just isn't an option. A traditional carlota is made with layers of Maria cookies (see Note, page 114) and a whipped lime and cream cheese filling, but I wanted to take it a step further by adding mango to the filling to give it more depth. The end result tastes just like a creamy mango paleta.

CARLOTA DE MANGO CON LIMÓN

Serves 8 to 10

12 ounces (340 g) diced mango

⅓ cup (77 g) fresh lime juice (about 3 limes)

1 cup (227 g) heavy cream

8 ounces (227 g) full-fat cream cheese, at room temperature

1 (14-ounce/397 g) can sweetened condensed milk

½ teaspoon vanilla bean paste

¼ teaspoon Diamond Crystal kosher salt or ⅛ teaspoon fine sea salt

12 ladyfingers, sliced in half crosswise, with a serrated knife

1 (4.9-ounce/139 g) sleeve of Maria cookies, sliced in half crosswise, with a serrated knife

+ In a blender, combine the mango and lime juice and blend on high speed until completely smooth, 45 seconds to 1 minute. Set the mango lime puree aside.

+ In a stand mixer fitted with the whisk, whip the heavy cream on medium-high speed until stiff peaks form. Scrape the finished whipped cream into a large bowl.

+ Swap out the whisk for the paddle attachment. In the same mixer bowl (no need to clean), beat the cream cheese on medium speed until it's nice and smooth, about 1 minute. Add the condensed milk, vanilla bean paste, and salt. Beat until everything has been fully incorporated, about 30 seconds. Scrape down the sides of the bowl. Pour in the mango lime puree, gradually bump the speed up to medium, and beat together for a full minute.

+ Take the bowl off the mixer and use a silicone spatula to carefully fold the whipped cream into the mango/cream cheese mixture, then set the filling aside.

+ Arrange the ladyfinger halves against the wall of a 9-inch (23 cm) springform pan, making sure the sugared sides of the cookies are facing out toward the wall, then use the Maria cookie halves to lay down a layer on the bottom of the pan. Carefully add 1 cup (250 g) of the mango filling and use a spoon or offset spatula to gently smooth it out. Repeat this process until you have about 4 layers of the Maria cookies, then top with the remaining filling.

+ Cover the top with plastic wrap and refrigerate overnight to set. The cake will be soft set, but if you'd like a cleaner and firmer slice, freeze for an hour or two before serving.

When I crave carrot cake, I imagine a moist and lightly spiced cake studded with walnuts and topped with a mountain of fluffy cream cheese frosting (because we love a good cake-to-frosting ratio). This recipe is exactly that. I've developed it so it yields enough batter for a two-layer cake—but also for one sheet cake, for those days when you just don't want to fuss with frosting and decorating a layer cake.

CLASSIC CARROT CAKE

Serves 8 to 10

FOR THE CAKE

2⅓ cups (291 g) unbleached all-purpose flour

1 tablespoon ground cinnamon

2 teaspoons baking soda

1 teaspoon Diamond Crystal kosher salt or ½ teaspoon fine sea salt

1 teaspoon ground ginger

¼ teaspoon ground cardamom

¼ teaspoon ground cloves

1½ cups (300 g) granulated sugar

⅔ cup lightly packed (139 g) light brown sugar

2 large eggs

1 cup (224 g) neutral oil (like canola or avocado)

¾ cup (172 g) buttermilk

3 cups (284 g) grated carrots (3 to 4 large carrots)

⅔ cup (86 g) walnuts, very finely chopped

FOR THE FROSTING

24 ounces (678 g) full-fat cream cheese, at room temperature

3 cups (300 g) powdered sugar

2 tablespoons heavy cream

2 teaspoons vanilla bean paste or extract

✦ **Make the cake:** Preheat the oven to 350°F (180°C). Lightly mist a 9 × 13-inch (23 × 33 cm) baking pan or two 8-inch (20 cm) round cake pans with cooking spray. If using round cake pans, line each bottom with a round of parchment paper and set aside.

✦ In a large bowl, whisk together the flour, cinnamon, baking soda, salt, ginger, cardamom, and cloves.

✦ In another large bowl, whisk together both sugars, the eggs, oil, and buttermilk until combined. Mix in the carrots and walnuts. Add the flour mixture all at once and use a silicone spatula to fold everything together just until combined.

✦ Scrape the batter into the baking pan or round cake pans (should be about 800 g of batter for each round cake pan). Bake just until a toothpick inserted into the center comes out clean, 40 to 45 minutes. Let the cake cool completely in the pan(s).

✦ **Make the frosting:** In a stand mixer fitted with the paddle, combine the cream cheese, heavy cream, and vanilla. Mix on slow to start then once it's combined, turn the speed up to medium and beat for a full minute until the cream cheese mixture is completely smooth. Reduce the speed to low then add in the powdered sugar, ½ cup (50 g) at a time. Once all of the powdered sugar has been incorporated, scrape down the sides of the bowl then beat on medium-low speed for about 30 seconds to one minute to make sure it's all combined.

✦ To frost the sheet cake, spread all of the frosting evenly over the top of the cake. Wrap with plastic wrap and refrigerate until ready to serve. To make the layer cake, place one of the cake layers upside down on a cake stand or serving platter, remove the parchment, and spread about 1 cup (235 g) of frosting evenly over the cake layer. Set the second layer on top, also upside down for a flat finished cake top, and remove the parchment from the second layer. Spread the remaining frosting evenly over the entire cake. Store in the refrigerator until ready to serve, but no longer than an hour to make sure the frosting doesn't dry out.

What's better than two new chocoflan recipes? Three new recipes! This chocoflan (well, there's technically no chocolate involved) gives off cozy and warm fall vibes with every bite. It has a layer of cream cheese flan and a very well spiced pumpkin cake.

SPICED PUMPKIN CHOCOFLAN

Serves 16

FOR THE BUNDT PAN

⅓ cup (100 g) dulce de leche or cajeta

FOR THE FLAN

1 (14-ounce/397 g) can sweetened condensed milk

1½ cups (354 g) half-and-half

8 ounces (227 grams) full-fat cream cheese, at room temperature

½ teaspoon pure vanilla extract

Pinch of salt

4 large eggs

FOR THE PUMPKIN CAKE

2 cups (250 g) unbleached all-purpose flour

1 teaspoon baking powder

1 teaspoon Diamond Crystal kosher salt or ½ teaspoon fine sea salt

½ teaspoon baking soda

1½ teaspoons ground cinnamon

½ teaspoon ground ginger

½ teaspoon freshly grated nutmeg or ¼ teaspoon ground nutmeg

(continues)

✦ Preheat the oven to 350°F (180°C). Mist a 10-cup Bundt pan (see Note on page 154) well with cooking spray. Cut out a piece of foil large enough to cover the top of the pan and mist it, too. Drizzle the dulce de leche into the bottom of the Bundt pan.

✦ **Make the flan:** In a blender, combine the condensed milk, half-and-half, cream cheese, vanilla, and salt. Blend for 1 minute on medium-high speed, then add the eggs and blend on medium-high for just about 10 seconds. Try not to blend for too long after you add the eggs so you don't whip too much air into the flan. Set this mixture aside.

✦ **Make the pumpkin cake:** In a large bowl, whisk together the flour, baking powder, salt, baking soda, cinnamon, ginger, nutmeg, and cardamom. In a second large bowl, whisk together the pumpkin puree, oil, buttermilk, and both sugars until you have a smooth mixture. Whisk in the eggs, one at a time, making sure not to overmix. Sift the dry ingredients into the bowl with the wet mixture, then use a rubber spatula to fold the dry into the wet. Scrape down the sides and bottom of the bowl to make sure everything is evenly incorporated.

✦ Scrape the cake batter into the prepared Bundt pan. Gently pour the flan over the top of it by pouring it into a ladle and letting it flow over the edge. This allows the flan to be added without disturbing the cake batter that much. If you aren't gentle when pouring the flan mixture over the batter, you'll have chunks of cake baking into the flan.

✦ Place the square of aluminum foil greased side down onto the Bundt pan and wrap it around the outside edge of the pan. No need to wrap it super tightly, but try not to just leave it sitting on top. Place the Bundt pan in a large roasting pan. Transfer the roasting pan to a pulled-out oven rack. Fill the roasting pan roughly two-thirds of the way up the sides with warm water (a large pitcher with a good spout is your best friend here) and close the oven door.

(continues)

¼ teaspoon ground cardamom

10 ounces (283 g) canned unsweetened pumpkin puree

⅓ cup (75 g) neutral oil (like vegetable or grapeseed)

¼ cup (57 g) buttermilk

1 cup (200 g) granulated sugar

⅓ cup (69 g) light brown sugar

2 large eggs

✦ Bake until a short bamboo skewer or cake tester comes out with only a few crumbs from the cake, 1 hour 45 minutes to 2 hours. Start checking on it at the 1 hour 45-minute mark and note that if the skewer goes into the flan its tip might be a little wet because the flan won't have set yet; it will do that in the refrigerator.

✦ Carefully remove the roasting pan from the oven and carefully lift the Bundt pan out of the water bath and place it on a cooling rack. Let the chocoflan cool completely at room temperature with the foil tented on top of the pan; this will take about 2 hours.

✦ Place the foil tightly back onto the pan and place the chocoflan in the refrigerator to set completely. This should take 4 to 5 hours, but an overnight 6- to 8-hour chill is ideal for the flan to set up perfectly.

✦ When you're ready to serve, carefully use the tips of your fingers to pull the cake away from the edge of the pan then place a large serving platter or cake stand over the Bundt pan and flip over to invert. Depending on your pan the chocoflan might be a little difficult to invert at first. If this is the case dip the bottom of the pan into a bowl of warm water for 5 to 6 minutes and try to invert the cake again.

✦ To store, carefully wrap it in plastic wrap and keep in the refrigerator for up to 3 days.

NOTE: I developed all of the chocoflan recipes using a basic Wilton Bundt pan. I noticed that when I used pans with more intricate designs, the baking time increased by 10 to 15 minutes, and that caused too much marbling. The simpler the Bundt pan, the easier it will be for the batters to swap places during the baking process.

I was introduced to baking through boxed cake and dessert mixes when I was in high school, and I often made no-bake Oreo cheesecake bars that my mom really enjoyed. These cookies and cream cheesecake bars have a crunchy chocolate crust, with a fluffy cream cheese and white chocolate filling and cookie bits throughout. They taste like those bars I once made, but better. For this recipe, you need to use white chocolate bars instead of white chocolate chips; the waxes and stabilizers in white chocolate chips make it hard to properly melt the chocolate down to be perfectly smooth and give the needed structure to the cheesecake. Look for good-quality white chocolate bars in the baking or candy aisles in the grocery store; they're usually sold in 4-ounce (113 g) bars.

NO-BAKE COOKIES AND CREAM CHEESECAKE BARS

Makes 16 bars

FOR THE CRUST

20 chocolate sandwich cookies

¼ cup (4 tablespoons/57 g) unsalted butter, melted

Pinch of salt

FOR THE FILLING

8 ounces (227 g) good-quality white chocolate, chopped

1 cup (227 g) cold heavy cream

1 pound (455 g) full-fat cream cheese, at room temperature, very soft

2 teaspoons pure vanilla extract

15 chocolate sandwich cookies, roughly chopped

✦ **Make the crust:** Mist an 8-inch (20 cm) square baking dish with cooking spray and place a piece of parchment in the pan to line the bottom and so that two sides hang over the edges of two sides.

✦ Place the 20 cookies in a food processor and process until you get something that looks like black sand. Measure out the crumbs to make sure you have 2 cups (230 g), then add them to a bowl. Sprinkle in a pinch of salt then add the melted butter and stir to combine. Press the crust carefully into the prepared pan; I like to use the bottom of a measuring cup or another flat surface like a drinking glass to press the crumbs into an even layer. Once the crust has been pressed in, place the pan in the refrigerator so the crust can firm up while you make the filling.

✦ **Make the filling:** Place the chocolate in a microwave-safe bowl and melt in 30-second bursts, stirring well after each 30 seconds. (Alternatively, melt in a double boiler; see Tip on page 157.) Set the bowl of melted chocolate aside to cool for a few minutes.

✦ In a stand mixer fitted with the whisk, whip the heavy cream until you have stiff peaks, making sure you don't overwhip and curdle the cream. Scrape the whipped cream into another bowl. Snap the paddle attachment onto the mixer. Add the cream cheese and vanilla to the bowl (no need to wash it out) and beat until light and fluffy, a full minute. Add all the melted white chocolate to the cream cheese and mix on medium speed until everything is evenly combined, about 30 seconds. Scrape down the sides of the bowl and mix again with a silicone spatula. Fold in all the whipped cream at once until it's just combined. Add the chopped chocolate sandwich cookies and fold them in, just enough to evenly distribute them.

(continues)

✦ Scrape the filling over the cookie base in the pan and smooth it out into an even layer. Cover the pan with plastic wrap and refrigerate for at least 4 hours. The filling will go from fluff to firm cheesecake consistency, like magic.

✦ When you're ready to serve, use the parchment overhang to lift the cheesecake out of the pan and place it on a cutting board to cut into slices.

TIP: To melt the chocolate in a double boiler, place the chocolate in a heatproof bowl that can sit partially over a saucepan of simmering water without touching the water. Bring 1 inch (2.5 cm) of water to a simmer, then set the bowl over the saucepan and stir occasionally until the chocolate is melted.

ANTOJITOS

When my husband, Billy, and I celebrated our first Christmas together back in 2011, we had just moved in with each other. I had started my first semester at Humboldt State up in NorCal earlier that fall, and it was taking me some time to adjust to the constant cold, misty, and gray weather. I often felt very out of place living there, especially since I could count the number of Mexican restaurants in town on a single hand, and the only grocery store that carried ingredients that I missed the most (like dried chiles and masa harina) was just a little liquor store on the side of Highway 101 at the entrance to town. It was a tiny space that felt like a safe haven to me. They had a small shelf with fresh pan dulce and a plethora of Mexican candies, and some space in their cooler for fresh Mexican cheeses. It was an oasis.

One of the things I taught Billy that Christmas was how to make tamales. His were double the size of mine (and spilling out of the husk), but he tried his best. I've always used food to help bring him into my culture, and getting to bond over tamales that first Christmas turned into a sweet memory that I'll cherish forever—and a moment we both get to have a laugh at every time Facebook brings up the picture of our tamales side by side.

SMALL BITES

These are traditional beef tamales made with a spicy chile guajillo sauce that I also like to sneak into the dough for more flavor. Although these tamales are made with beef, you can easily swap it out for pork or chicken.

TAMALES DE RES CON CHILE ROJO
Red Beef Tamales

Makes about 18 tamales

24 large dried corn husks

FOR THE FILLING

12 large guajillo chiles, stemmed and seeded

2 ancho chiles, stemmed and seeded

1½ teaspoons apple cider vinegar

6 garlic cloves, peeled

1 teaspoon black peppercorns

1 teaspoon dried Mexican oregano

½ teaspoon cumin seeds

1½ teaspoons fresh thyme leaves

2½ teaspoons Diamond Crystal kosher salt or 1¼ teaspoons fine sea salt, plus more to taste

2½ pounds (1.1 kg) beef chuck roast, cut into 3-inch (7.5 cm) cubes

1 bay leaf

3½ cups (826 g) low-sodium beef stock

(continues)

✦ **Rehydrate the corn husks:** Place the corn husks in a large heatproof bowl, then cover with hot water and let sit for at least 15 minutes.

✦ **Make the filling:** In a medium saucepan, combine the guajillos and anchos and add enough water to cover by 1 inch (2.5 cm). Bring the water to a boil, then reduce the heat to low and let cook for 15 minutes. Drain the softened chiles into a sieve set over a bowl to catch the chile soaking liquid. Measure 3½ cups (826 g) of the chile soaking liquid; if you don't have enough, add water until you do.

✦ Transfer the chiles to a blender, then add the apple cider vinegar, garlic, peppercorns, Mexican oregano, cumin seeds, thyme, salt, and reserved chile soaking liquid. Blend until smooth. Taste the sauce for salt and adjust. Measure out 1 cup (228 g) of the chile puree and set aside, as you'll use it for the dough. Pour the rest of the chile puree into a large dutch oven. Add the beef cubes, bay leaf, and beef stock, stir, then cover and bring to a boil over medium heat. Once it reaches a boil, reduce the heat to low and cook until the beef shreds easily, 3 to 3½ hours.

✦ Use a slotted spoon to remove the beef, then use two forks to shred. Toss out the bay leaf, then increase the heat under the dutch oven to medium and cook to reduce the sauce for 12 to 15 minutes. Remove from the heat. Taste the sauce for salt and adjust. Return the shredded beef to the sauce and toss to coat.

✦ **Make the masa:** In a large bowl, whisk together the masa harina, baking powder, and salt. Add the lard to a stand mixer fitted with the paddle and whip the lard for 2½ minutes on medium speed. Reduce the speed to low, then alternate between adding the masa harina (¼ cup/28 g at a time) and the reserved 1 cup (228 g) chile puree. Once all of the masa harina has been incorporated, pour in the beef stock in a slow and steady stream.

(continues)

FOR THE MASA

4 cups (448 g) Maseca masa harina (for tortillas)

2½ teaspoons baking powder

1½ teaspoons Diamond Crystal kosher salt or ¾ teaspoon fine sea salt

1¼ cups (260 g) lard

2½ cups (590 g) low-sodium beef stock

Turn the mixer off, then use a rubber spatula to scrape down the sides and bottom of the bowl. Gradually bump the speed up to medium-low and beat for 30 seconds. Cover the bowl with plastic wrap and let the dough sit for 20 minutes to fully hydrate.

✦ To assemble the tamales, reserve 18 corn husks for the tamales and take a couple of extra husks and rip them into 36 strips ¼ inch (6 mm) wide and 8 inches (20 cm) long. Take 2 strips and tie them together at the ends, until you're left with 18 strips 14 to 15 inches (35 to 38 cm) long. You'll use these to tie the tamales.

✦ Grab a large corn husk and add about ⅓ cup (85 g) of the dough. Use a spoon, offset spatula, or wet fingers to spread the masa down into a square, leaving 1 inch (2.5 cm) of space on the top, left, and right sides and at least 3 to 4 inches (7.5 to 10 cm) of space on the bottom. Add 2 tablespoons of the filling to the center, then fold the right edge of the masa over to meet the left edge and press the edges down to seal. Tuck the left side of the husk into the right side, then wrap the right side of the husk around to create a tube, then fold the bottom upward. The top of the tamal stays open. Tie a strip around the bottom of the tamal, to secure the bottom fold, then repeat the process with the remaining tamales. As you work, place the tamales vertically in a steamer insert, open side up.

✦ Add 1½ quarts (1.5 liters) water to a steamer pot. Add the steamer insert, cover, and bring the water to a boil (10 to 12 minutes). Reduce the heat to medium-low and steam until the masa cleanly pulls away from the husk, 1 hour 25 minutes to 1 hour 40 minutes. At the 1-hour mark, check the bottom of the pot for water and replenish as needed. If the water for the steam runs out, the bottom of the pot will burn and get ruined.

✦ Store in an airtight container or gallon-sized resealable plastic bag. These tamales will keep for 4 days max in the fridge, and 3 to 4 weeks in the freezer. The freshness and flavor start to decline past this. To reheat, steam for 30 to 40 minutes until fully warmed through.

Tamales de elote are sweet tamales made with sweet white corn. I like to add a touch of butter and honey to mine because they complement each other so well! This recipe relies on the sweetness of the corn for flavor, so if it isn't in season, use frozen. Just let the frozen corn thaw, and drain any excess liquid. You can eat these tamales on their own, but I find they're perfect with a glass of milk.

TAMALES DE ELOTE
Sweet Corn Tamales

Makes 12 tamales

18 large dried corn husks

FOR THE MASA

5 cups (750 g) sweet white corn kernels (from about 6 large ears corn)

¼ cup (59 g) milk

1⅓ cups (149 g) Maseca masa harina (for tortillas)

1½ teaspoons baking powder

1 teaspoon Diamond Crystal kosher salt or ½ teaspoon fine sea salt

½ cup (8 tablespoons/115 g) unsalted butter, at room temperature

½ cup (100 g) granulated sugar

⅓ cup (112 g) honey

✦ Place the corn husks in a large heatproof bowl. Cover with hot water and let sit for at least 15 minutes.

✦ In a blender, blend together the corn kernels and milk on high speed until you have a smooth puree, 25 to 30 seconds. Set aside.

✦ In a large bowl, whisk together the masa harina, baking powder, and salt. In a stand mixer fitted with the paddle, beat together the butter, sugar, and honey for 2½ minutes on medium speed. Bump the speed down to low and alternate between adding the corn puree and the flour mixture, until everything has been incorporated.

✦ Turn the mixer off and use a rubber spatula to scrape down the sides and bottom of the bowl. Slowly bump the speed up to medium-low and beat for 30 seconds, then cover the bowl with plastic wrap and let the dough sit for 20 minutes to fully hydrate.

✦ Once the corn husks are rehydrated and pliable, reserve 12 of them for the tamales, then take a couple of the extra husks and rip 24 strips ¼ inch (6 mm) wide and 8 inches long. Tie two together until you have 12 strips 15 to 16 inches (38 to 40 cm) long. You'll use these to tie the tamales.

✦ To assemble the tamales, grab a corn husk and place it in the palm of your hand, then use a spoon to add a heaping ⅓ cup (100 g) of the dough to the center of the husk, leaving 1 inch (2.5 cm) of free space on the top, left, and right sides and at least 3 to 4 inches (7.5 to 10 cm) on the bottom. The dough will expand as it cooks, so if you don't leave some empty space for clearance at the top, it will ooze out.

✦ Fold the right edge of the husk over the dough toward the left side, then take the left side of the husk and fold it over the right side to create a tube, then fold the bottom flap upward (leaving the top open). Tie a strip around the bottom of the tamal, to secure the bottom fold. As you work, place the tamales vertically in a steamer insert, open side up, making sure not to crowd the steamer insert.

(continues)

✦ Add 1½ quarts (1.5 liters) water to a steamer pot. Add the steamer insert, cover, and bring the water to a boil (10 to 15 minutes). Reduce the heat to medium-low and steam for 1 hour 20 minutes to 1 hour 40 minutes. At the 1-hour mark, check the bottom of the pot for water and replenish as needed. If the water for the steam runs out, the bottom of the pot will burn and get ruined.

✦ It's tricky to tell when sweet tamales are done cooking because they're soft while they're steaming but firm up once cooled; on average these tamales take 1 hour 30 minutes to fully cook. You can start checking for doneness at the 1 hour 20-minute mark. Simply take a tamal out, let it cool for 8 to 10 minutes, then check the inside. If the center looks raw or soft set, continue to let the tamales steam for another 10 to 20 minutes.

✦ Store in an airtight container or gallon-sized resealable plastic bag. The tamales will keep for 4 days max in the fridge, and 3 to 4 weeks in the freezer. The freshness and flavor start to decline past this. To reheat, steam for 20 to 30 minutes over medium-low heat until fully warmed through.

NOTE: This isn't necessary, but to ensure that no steam or condensation gets into each tamal, I like to take a second corn husk, wrap it around the top of the tamal, then fold down and tie it around the center to secure. If you include this step, you will need to have 30 dried corn husks.

Enfrijoladas consist of corn tortillas that are lightly fried, dipped in a black bean sauce, and then stuffed with quesillo (queso Oaxaca), and topped with crispy chorizo. They are one of my favorite comfort foods and one of my favorite ways to use tortillas and leftover beans. If you don't feel like making a batch of stovetop beans, you can save yourself some time by using canned beans—I promise you won't lose any flavor! Serve with rice and beans, or on their own.

ENFRIJOLADAS

Serves 3 or 4

FOR THE FILLING

2 tablespoons vegetable oil

1 small yellow onion, diced

1 small carrot, finely diced

2 celery stalks, diced

1 green bell pepper, diced

3 chiles de árbol, stems and
    seeds removed

5 garlic cloves, minced

¾ teaspoon ground cumin

¾ teaspoon ground coriander

3 (15-ounce/425 g) cans black
    beans, drained

2½ cups (590 g) low-sodium
    chicken stock

12 ounces (340 g) chorizo or
    longaniza, casings removed

FOR ASSEMBLY

12 corn tortillas

1 cup (224 g) vegetable oil

6 cups (672 g) shredded
    queso Oaxaca (or substitute
    mozzarella)

Diced white onion

Chopped fresh cilantro

✦ **Make the filling:** In a large skillet, heat the vegetable oil over medium heat. Add the onion, carrot, celery, and bell pepper and sauté until the onion becomes translucent, 6 to 7 minutes. Add the chiles de árbol, garlic, cumin, and coriander and sauté until the garlic becomes fragrant, 5 more minutes.

✦ Remove the veggies from the heat. Use a slotted spoon to transfer them to a blender. Add the black beans, then pour in the chicken stock. Blend until smooth, 45 seconds to 1 minute. I like the bean sauce to be a little thicker, but if you'd like to thin it out slightly, add up to an extra ¾ cup (180 g) chicken stock.

✦ Transfer the sauce to a medium saucepan, taste for salt, and adjust, then place it over low heat. Stir occasionally to make sure the bottom doesn't burn. The black bean sauce needs to stay warm, or the cheese won't melt.

✦ Wipe the large skillet clean, set over medium heat, add the chorizo, and use a silicone spatula to break it up into smaller chunks. Cook until crispy and all the fat has rendered, 10 to 12 minutes. Transfer the chorizo to a plate lined with paper towels to drain, then wipe the skillet clean.

✦ **To assemble:** Pop the tortillas in the microwave for 30 seconds. Set the large skillet over medium heat, add the oil, and heat until hot and shimmery. Add 1 to 2 tortillas at a time and fry for 45 seconds to 1 minute on each side. They should be lightly fried, but still pliable so they don't get soggy as soon as you dip them into the black bean sauce. Let the tortillas drain on a plate lined with paper towels and replenish the oil as needed.

✦ For each enfrijolada, use a pair of tongs to dip a tortilla into the black bean sauce, then stuff with ¼ cup (28 g) of the shredded cheese. Fold to close. Top with another ¼ cup (28 g) shredded cheese, then sprinkle a couple of tablespoons of the crispy chorizo on top. Finish with a sprinkling of diced onion and chopped cilantro. Continue to assemble the remaining enfrijoladas: I like to serve 3 to 4 per plate.

Picaditas were one of my favorite things mi abuelita Victoria used to make for me whenever she ordered fresh masa for sopitos. The picaditas she used to make me consisted of large sopes with fresh salsa roja or salsa de molcajete, diced onions, and fresh queso Cotija. I'm including a recipe for a quick mild salsa roja, but you can use whatever kind of salsa you have left over in your refrigerator.

PICADITAS

Makes 12 picaditas

FOR THE SALSA ROJA

1 pound (454 g) Roma tomatoes, sliced in half horizontally

2 Mexican spring onions or 4 green onions

3 chiles de árbol

4 garlic cloves, peeled

1 teaspoon Diamond Crystal kosher salt or ½ teaspoon fine sea salt, plus more to taste

FOR THE SOPES

2 cups (224 g) Maseca masa harina (for tortillas)

1 teaspoon Diamond Crystal kosher salt or ½ teaspoon fine sea salt

1½ cups (354 g) hot water

FOR ASSEMBLY

Crema Mexicana

Diced white onion

Chopped fresh cilantro

Grated queso Cotija

✦ **Make the salsa roja:** Preheat the broiler to high. Line a baking sheet with foil.

✦ Arrange the tomatoes skin side up on the baking sheet along with the onions. Broil until the veggies have a nice and even char on top, about 15 minutes. Set them aside to cool.

✦ Meanwhile, place a small skillet over medium heat. Once it comes up to temperature, add the chiles de árbol and cook for 30 to 45 seconds on each side, just until they start to darken, then remove them from the heat, remove the stems, and set aside.

✦ Once cooled, throw the broiled tomatoes, onions, chiles de árbol, garlic cloves, and the salt into a blender and blend on high for 30 to 45 seconds until smooth. Pour the salsa into a bowl, taste for salt, then adjust.

✦ **Make the sopes:** In a large bowl, whisk together the masa harina and salt. Pour in the hot water about ¼ cup (60 g) at a time and use your hands to incorporate it. Once all the water has been incorporated and you have a smooth round ball of dough, cover the bowl with plastic wrap and let the dough hydrate for 20 minutes.

✦ Divide the dough into 12 equal portions (about 45 g each) and roll into balls. Make sure to keep any dough you're not using covered, to prevent it from drying out.

✦ Place a large cast-iron or nonstick skillet or comal over high heat.

✦ Grab a 1-gallon (4-liter) resealable plastic bag and cut it at the seams so you have two separate squares. Place one of the squares on the bottom plate of the tortilla press, then place a ball of dough on top of it, then cover with the second plastic square and close and press down to flatten the dough into a 5-inch (12 cm) disc.

✦ Gently peel off the top plastic square, then flip the disc onto your palm and gently peel off the remaining plastic square. Place the dough onto the hot skillet and cook for 30 seconds, flip and cook for another 30 seconds, then flip and cook for 30 seconds, then flip once more and cook for 30 more seconds. Use a spatula to remove the cooked sope and transfer it to a clean surface. Working quickly, while the sope is still hot, use your fingers to carefully pinch the edges of the sope up to create a wall around the perimeter, making sure you don't rip the sope, as this wall will hold in the salsa. Place the finished sopes in a bowl and cover with a kitchen towel to let the residual steam finish cooking them.

✦ To assemble a picadita, take a sope, top with 2 to 3 tablespoons of the salsa, then garnish with a drizzle of crema Mexicana, diced white onion, chopped cilantro, and a sprinkling of Cotija.

Chochoyotes are one of my favorite things to make with masa harina. They are small round Mexican dumplings made with corn masa that have a crater in the center, typically made for soups. I love adding them to a rich crema de frijol (black bean soup) for a full meal, but they also pair well with other brothy soups and moles.

CREMA DE FRIJOL CON CHOCHOYOTES

Serves 4 to 5

FOR THE CHOCHOYOTES

1⅔ cups (186 g) Maseca masa harina (for tortillas)

1 teaspoon Diamond Crystal kosher salt or ½ teaspoon fine sea salt

2 tablespoons lard or vegetable shortening

1 cup (236 g) hot water

FOR THE SOUP

2 tablespoons neutral cooking oil, such as vegetable or avocado oil

1 large yellow onion, chopped

2 celery stalks, chopped

1 green bell pepper, chopped

6 garlic cloves, minced

2 chiles de árbol, stems removed

⅓ cup fresh cilantro leaves, minced

¾ teaspoon ground cumin

12 ounces (340 g) chorizo (or longaniza)

3 cups cooked black beans or 2 (15-ounce/425 g) cans black beans, drained and rinsed

4 cups (944 g) low-sodium chicken or vegetable stock

4 tablespoons crema Mexicana, plus more for drizzling

Kosher salt or fine sea salt

Crumbled queso fresco, for serving

Chopped cilantro, for garnish

✦ **Make the chochoyotes:** In a large bowl mix the masa harina and salt. Work in the lard with your fingertips until incorporated. Add the hot water and mix until combined. Use a tablespoon to scoop out the dough, rolling it between your hands to make a smooth ball. Use a thumb to make a crater in the center to help the dumplings cook evenly. Place the chochoyotes on a baking sheet, covering with a damp towel as you form them. To prepare to cook the chochoyotes, fill a wide shallow pot with a few inches of water and bring to a simmer. Leave the chochoyotes covered on the baking sheet while you make the soup.

✦ **Make the soup:** In a large dutch oven or stockpot, heat the oil over medium-low heat. Add the onion, celery, bell pepper, garlic, chiles, cilantro, and cumin. Cook until the vegetables have cooked down significantly and are very soft, 10 to 15 minutes.

✦ Meanwhile, in a sauté pan, crisp up the chorizo over medium heat. Once crumbled into smaller pieces, set aside.

✦ Add the black beans and stock to the dutch oven and bring to a simmer. Cook for 20 minutes to combine.

✦ While the soup simmers, cook the chochoyotes. Reduce the heat under the pot of water to just below a simmer. Gently add the chochoyotes and cook 12 to 15 minutes. Scoop out a chochoyote and cut it open to check for doneness.

✦ After the soup has simmered for 20 minutes, use an immersion blender to blend to your desired consistency. Stir in the crema and taste for salt.

✦ Serve with a few chochoyotes, a few tablespoons of crispy chorizo, and an extra drizzle of crema Mexicana, crumbled queso fresco, and chopped cilantro.

Tamales verdes were probably my favorite tamales growing up! They consist of corn dough filled with shredded chicken braised in a tangy salsa verde. This recipe calls for chicken, but you can substitute pork; just make sure to cook the pork for 3 to 3½ hours until it shreds easily.

TAMALES DE CHILE VERDE CON POLLO
Chicken Chile Verde Tamales

Makes about 18 tamales

30 large dried corn husks

FOR THE FILLING

2 pounds (907 g) tomatillos, husked, rinsed, and halved

1 poblano pepper, halved, seeded, and stem removed

1 onion, quartered

6 garlic cloves, peeled

3 serrano chiles, stemmed and halved

¼ cup (10 g) fresh cilantro leaves

Juice of ½ lime

2½ teaspoons Diamond Crystal kosher salt or 1¼ teaspoons fine sea salt, plus more to taste

1 teaspoon dried Mexican oregano

¾ teaspoon ground cumin

¼ teaspoon freshly ground black pepper

2 cups (472 g) low-sodium chicken stock

2½ pounds (1.1 kg) boneless, skinless chicken thighs

(continues)

✦ **Rehydrate the corn husks:** Place the corn husks in a large heatproof bowl, then cover with hot water and let sit for at least 15 minutes.

✦ **Make the filling:** Preheat the broiler. Line a baking sheet with foil.

✦ Arrange the tomatillos, poblano (skin side up), and onion quarters on the sheet. Broil until everything has an even char, 12 to 15 minutes. Let the veggies cool for 20 minutes. Then use your fingers to remove the waxy outer skin from the poblanos.

✦ In a blender or food processor, combine the tomatillos, poblano, onion, garlic, serranos, cilantro, lime juice, salt, oregano, cumin, and black pepper, and the ½ cup (118 g) of chicken stock and blend until smooth. Measure out 1 cup (225 g) of the salsa verde and set aside.

✦ Add the chicken thighs to a large dutch oven or stockpot, pour in the remaining salsa verde, then stir in the 1½ cups (354 g) chicken stock. Bring to a boil over medium heat, then reduce the heat to medium-low, cover, and braise until the chicken shreds easily, 1 hour to 1 hour 10 minutes.

✦ Use a slotted spoon to remove the chicken and use two forks to shred. Increase the heat under the pot to medium and let the sauce reduce uncovered for 12 minutes. Remove from the heat. Taste the sauce for salt and adjust, then toss the shredded chicken back into the sauce.

✦ **Make the masa:** In a large bowl, whisk together the masa harina, baking powder, and salt. In a stand mixer fitted with the paddle, whip the lard on medium speed until fluffy and pale, about 2½ minutes. Reduce the speed to low, then alternate between sprinkling in the masa harina mixture ¼ cup (28 g) at a time and the reserved 1 cup (225 g) salsa verde. Once all of the reserved salsa verde has been incorporated, pour in the chicken stock in a slow and steady stream. Turn the mixer off and use a rubber

(continues)

FOR THE MASA

4 cups (448 g) Maseca masa harina (for tortillas)

2½ teaspoons baking powder

1½ teaspoons Diamond Crystal kosher salt or ¾ teaspoon fine sea salt

1¼ cups (260 g) lard

2¼ cups (531 g) low-sodium chicken stock

spatula to scrape down the sides and bottom of the bowl. Slowly bring the speed up to medium-low and beat for 30 seconds, taste the masa for salt, and adjust, then cover the bowl with plastic wrap and let the dough sit for 20 minutes to fully hydrate.

✦ To assemble the tamales, reserve 18 of the corn husks. Take a couple of the extra husks and rip 36 strips ¼ inch (6 mm) wide and 8 inches (20 cm) long. Take 2 strips and tie them together at the ends, until you're left with 18 strips 14 to 15 inches (35 to 38 cm) long. You'll use these to tie the tamales.

✦ Grab a large corn husk and add about ⅓ cup (85 g) of the masa. Use a spoon, offset spatula, or wet fingers to spread the masa down into a square, leaving 1 inch (2.5 cm) of space on the top, left, and right sides and at least 3 to 4 inches (7.5 to 10 cm) of space on the bottom. Add 2 tablespoons of the filling in the center, then fold the right edge of the masa over to meet the left edge and press the edges down to seal. Tuck the left side of the husk into the right side, then wrap the right side of the husk around to create a tube, and fold the bottom upward (leaving the top open). Tie a strip around the bottom of the tamal, to secure the bottom fold. As you work, place the tamales vertically in a steamer insert, open side up, making sure not to crowd the steamer insert.

✦ Add 1½ quarts (1.5 liters) water to a steamer pot. Add the steamer insert, cover, and bring the water to a boil (10 to 12 minutes). Reduce the heat to medium-low and steam until the masa cleanly pulls away from the husk, 1 hour 25 minutes to 1 hour 40 minutes. At the 1-hour mark, check the bottom of the pot for water, and replenish as needed. If the water for the steam runs out, the bottom of the pot will burn and get ruined.

✦ Store in an airtight container or gallon-sized resealable plastic bag. The tamales will keep for 4 days max in the fridge, and 3 to 4 weeks in the freezer. The freshness and flavor start to decline past this. To reheat, steam for 30 to 40 minutes over medium-low heat until fully warmed through.

Slices of poblano peppers or jalapeños are often referred to as *rajas*, or "slices," which is exactly what we use for the filling in these tamales! Tamales de rajas con queso consist of corn dough stuffed with slices of melty mozzarella and panela cheese along with poblano pepper and a spicy salsa verde.

TAMALES DE RAJAS CON QUESO
Rajas con Queso Tamales

Makes about 18 tamales

24 large dried corn husks

FOR THE SALSA VERDE

1½ pounds tomatillos, husked, rinsed, and halved

4 large poblano peppers (use 6 to 8 for more heat)

3 Mexican green onions or 5 regular green onions

6 garlic cloves, peeled

2 serrano chiles, stemmed and seeded

¼ cup (10 g) fresh cilantro leaves

Juice of ½ lime

1½ teaspoons Diamond Crystal kosher salt, plus more to taste

FOR THE MASA

4 cups (448 g) Maseca masa harina (for tortillas)

2½ teaspoons baking powder

1½ teaspoons Diamond Crystal kosher salt or ¾ teaspoon fine sea salt

1¼ cups (260 g) lard or vegetable shortening

2¼ cups (531 g) low-sodium chicken stock or vegetable stock

(continues)

✦ **Rehydrate the corn husks:** Place the corn husks in a large heatproof bowl, then cover with hot water and let sit for at least 15 minutes.

✦ **Make the salsa verde:** Preheat the broiler. Line a baking sheet with foil.

✦ Place the tomatillos skin side up on the baking sheet and add the poblanos. Broil until they all have an even char, 12 to 15 minutes, flipping the poblanos halfway through.

✦ Place the poblano peppers in a bowl, cover with plastic wrap, and let steam for 10 to 15 minutes. While the peppers steam, in a blender or food processor, combine the tomatillos, green onions, garlic, serranos, cilantro, lime juice, and salt and blend until smooth. Measure out 1 cup (250 g) of the salsa verde and set aside for the masa.

✦ Once the peppers are done steaming, use your fingers to remove the waxy skin, then remove the seeds and stems and slice into long strips (rajas) ¼ inch (6 mm) wide.

✦ **Make the masa:** In a large bowl, whisk together the masa harina, baking powder, and salt. In a stand mixer fitted with the paddle, whip the lard for 2½ minutes on medium speed. Reduce the speed to low, then alternate between adding the masa harina ¼ cup (28 g) at a time and the 1 cup (250 g) salsa verde. Once all of the masa harina has been incorporated, pour in the chicken stock in a slow and steady stream. Turn the mixer off and use a rubber spatula to scrape down the sides and bottom of the bowl. Slowly bump the speed up to medium-low and beat for 30 seconds, taste the masa for salt and adjust, then cover the bowl with plastic wrap and let the dough sit for 20 minutes to fully hydrate.

(continues)

FOR ASSEMBLY

18 ounces (510 g) mozzarella cheese, cut into 18 sticks ½ inch (1.25 cm) thick and 3 to 4 inches (7.5 to 10 cm) long

18 ounces (510 g) panela cheese, sliced into 18 sticks ½ inch (1.25 cm) thick and 3 to 4 inches (7.5 to 10 cm) long

✦ **Assemble the tamales:** Take a couple of corn husks and rip them into 18 strips ¼ inch (6 mm) wide. You'll use these to tie the tamales. Grab a soaked corn husk and add ⅓ cup (about 85 g) of the masa. Use wet fingers or an offset spatula to spread the masa down into a rectangle, leaving 1 inch (2.5 cm) of space on the top, left, and right sides and at least 3 to 4 inches (7.5 to 10 cm) on the bottom. Add about 1 tablespoon of the salsa verde to the center, then add 2 to 3 poblano strips followed by 1 strip each of mozzarella and panela. Fold the right edge of the tamal over to meet the left edge and press the edges down to seal. Tuck the left side of the husk into the right side, to create a tube, then fold the bottom upward (leaving the top open). Tie a strip around the bottom of the tamal to secure the bottom fold, then repeat the process with the remaining tamales. As you work, place the tamales vertically in a steamer insert, open side up, making sure not to crowd the steamer insert.

✦ Add 1½ quarts (1.5 liters) water to a steamer pot. Add the steamer insert, cover, and bring the water to a boil (10 to 12 minutes). Reduce the heat to medium-low and steam until the masa cleanly pulls away from the husk, 1 hour 20 minutes to 1 hour 30 minutes. At the 1-hour mark, check the bottom of the pot for water and replenish as needed. If the water for the steam runs out, the bottom of the pot will burn and get ruined.

✦ Store in an airtight container or gallon-sized resealable plastic bag. These tamales will keep for 4 days max in the fridge, and 3 to 4 weeks in the freezer. The freshness and flavor start to decline past this. To reheat, steam for 20 to 30 minutes over medium-low heat until fully warmed through.

Molletes are toasty slices of bolillo or telera rolls with a layer of refried beans, melty cheese, and crispy chorizo, topped with a fresh pico de gallo and crumbled queso Cotija. They make for a good breakfast and are a perfect way to use up any leftover beans or rolls from the night before.

MOLLETES

Makes 6 slices

12 ounces (340 g) chorizo (or longaniza), casings removed

1 to 2 tablespoons neutral oil, such as canola or avocado

3 telera rolls, sliced in half horizontally (you can also use bolillos)

FOR THE PICO DE GALLO

¾ cup (340 g) diced Roma tomatoes (from 4 or 5)

¼ white onion, diced

¼ cup (10 g) finely chopped fresh cilantro

1 serrano chile, thinly sliced

Pinch of salt

Juice of ½ lime

FOR ASSEMBLY

1¼ (325 g) cups refried beans

1¼ cups (140 g) shredded mozzarella

Crumbled queso Cotija

Crema Mexicana, for drizzling

✦ In a large skillet, cook the chorizo over medium heat, breaking it up into smaller chunks, until the fat has rendered and the chorizo is nice and crispy, 10 to 12 minutes. Use a slotted spoon to transfer to a plate lined with a paper towel to drain.

✦ Add 1 tablespoon of the neutral oil to the pan and place 2 to 3 telera halves cut side down in the skillet and toast until golden, about 1 minute. Repeat with the remaining split rolls and add another tablespoon of oil if needed.

✦ **Make the pico de gallo:** In a medium bowl, stir together the tomatoes, onion, cilantro, serrano, salt, and lime juice. Set aside.

✦ **To assemble:** Preheat the broiler to high. Line a baking sheet with parchment paper.

✦ Spread 2 to 3 tablespoons of refried beans over each roll half, then transfer to the lined pan. Add 2 tablespoons of the chorizo over the beans, then sprinkle 3 tablespoons of shredded mozzarella on top. Broil the slices of bread until the cheese is nice and melted, 1 to 2 minutes.

✦ Let cool for 2 minutes, then serve each slice with 3 tablespoons of the pico de gallo, crumbled Cotija, and a drizzle of crema Mexicana.

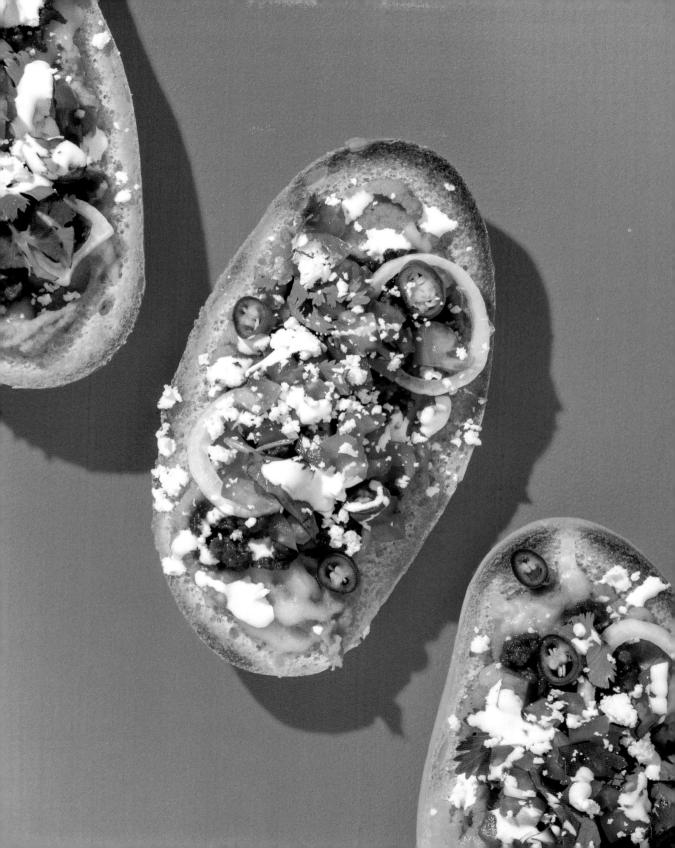

Tamales de piña are one of the sweet tamales you're likely to encounter at a posada or my mom's house during the Christmas season, and they pair so well with Coconut Atole (page 196). Be sure to use a fresh pineapple for these tamales; fresh pineapple always provides better flavor than canned.

TAMALES DE PIÑA
Sweet Pineapple Tamales

Makes 12 tamales

18 large dried corn husks

1 pound (454g) fresh pineapple chunks

½ cup (118 g) pineapple juice

1¾ cups (196 g) Maseca masa harina (for tortillas)

1½ teaspoons baking powder

1 teaspoon Diamond Crystal kosher salt or ½ teaspoon fine sea salt

½ cup (8 tablespoons/115 g) unsalted butter, at room temperature

½ cup (104 g) light brown sugar

⅓ cup (112 g) honey

→ Rehydrate the corn husks by placing them in a large heatproof bowl, covering with hot water, and letting sit for at least 15 minutes.

→ In a blender, combine the pineapple chunks and pineapple juice and blend on high speed until you have a smooth puree, 30 to 40 seconds. Set aside.

→ In a large bowl, whisk together the masa harina, baking powder, and salt. In a stand mixer fitted with the paddle, combine the butter, brown sugar, and honey and beat together for 2½ minutes on medium speed. Reduce the speed to low, then alternate between adding in the masa harina ¼ cup (28 g) at a time and the pineapple puree, until everything has been incorporated. Turn the mixer off, then use a rubber spatula to scrape down the sides and bottom of the bowl. Gradually bring the speed up to medium-low and beat for 30 seconds. Cover the bowl with plastic wrap and let the dough sit for 20 minutes to fully hydrate.

→ Once the corn husks are rehydrated and pliable, reserve 12 of them for the tamales, then take a couple of the extra husks and rip 24 strips ¼ inch (6 mm) wide and 8 inches long. Tie two together until you have 12 strips 15 to 16 inches (38 to 40 cm) long. You'll use these to tie the tamales.

→ To assemble the tamales, grab a corn husk and place it in the palm of your hand. Use a spoon to add about a heaping ⅓ cup (110 g) of the dough to the center of the husk, leaving 1 inch (2.5 cm) free space on the top, left, and right sides and at least 3 to 4 inches (7.5 to 10 cm) of space on the bottom. The dough will expand as it cooks, so if you don't leave the inch of empty space for clearance at the top, it will ooze out.

→ Fold the right edge of the husk over the dough toward the left side, then take the left side of the husk and fold it over the right side to create a tube, then fold the bottom flap upward (leaving the top open). Tie a strip around the bottom of the tamal, to secure the bottom fold. As you work, place the folded tamales upright inside a steamer insert, making sure not to crowd the steamer insert.

(continues)

✦ Add 1½ quarts (1.5 liters) water to a steamer pot. Add the steamer insert, cover, and bring the water to a boil (10 to 15 minutes). Reduce the heat to medium-low and steam for 1 hour 35 minutes to 1 hour 45 minutes. At the 1-hour mark, check the bottom of the pot for water and replenish as needed. If the water for the steam runs out, the bottom of the pot will burn and get ruined.

✦ It's tricky to tell when sweet tamales are done cooking because they're soft while they're steaming but firm up once cooled; on average these tamales take about 1 hour 40 minutes to fully cook. You can start checking for doneness at the 1 hour 25-minute mark. Simply take a tamal out and let it cool for 8 to 10 minutes, then check the inside. If the center looks a little raw or soft, continue to let the tamales steam for another 10 to 20 minutes.

✦ Store in an airtight container or gallon-sized resealable plastic bag. These tamales will keep for 4 days max in the fridge, and 3 to 4 weeks in the freezer. The freshness and flavor starts to decline past this. To reheat, steam for 20 to 30 minutes over medium-low heat until fully warmed through.

NOTE: This isn't necessary, but to ensure that no steam or condensation gets into each tamal, I like to take a second corn husk, wrap it around the top of the tamal, fold down and tie it around the center to secure.

Tamales de fresa are one of my favorite things to make during berry season! Although these tamales call for strawberries, feel free to use any combination of berries that might be in season, as long as their weight totals 1¼ pounds (570 g). Strawberries have a subtle flavor, so using ripe strawberries will yield a more flavorful tamal. If you are making these tamales and strawberries aren't in season anymore, use frozen, because frozen fruit is picked when it is ripe. Just let the berries thaw and drain any excess liquid.

TAMALES DE FRESA
Sweet Strawberry Tamales

Makes 12 tamales

24 large dried corn husks

FOR THE FILLING

⅓ cup (79 g) boiling water

1 tablespoon dried hibiscus

1¼ pounds (570 g) strawberries

½ cup (60 g) agave nectar or honey

FOR THE MASA

1¾ cups (196 g) Maseca masa harina (for tortillas)

1½ teaspoons baking powder

1 teaspoon Diamond Crystal kosher salt or ½ teaspoon fine sea salt

½ cup (8 tablespoons/115 g) unsalted butter, room temperature

⅓ cup (66 g) sugar

✦ Rehydrate the corn husks by placing them in a large heatproof bowl, covering with hot water, and letting sit for at least 15 minutes.

✦ **Make the filling:** In a small heatproof bowl, combine the boiling water and the dried hibiscus and let steep for 20 minutes.

✦ After 20 minutes, strain the hibiscus tea into a blender, then add the strawberries and agave nectar and blend on medium-high speed for 1 minute, until you have a smooth puree.

✦ **Make the masa:** In a large bowl, whisk together the masa harina, baking powder, and salt. In a stand mixer fitted with the paddle, beat the butter and sugar together for 2½ minutes on medium speed. Reduce the speed to low, then alternate between adding the masa harina ¼ cup (28 g) at a time and the strawberry puree, until everything has been incorporated. Turn the mixer off, then use a rubber spatula to scrape down the sides and bottom of the bowl. Gradually bring the speed up to medium-low and beat for 30 seconds. Cover the bowl with plastic wrap and let the dough sit for 20 minutes to fully hydrate.

✦ Once the corn husks are rehydrated and pliable, reserve 12 of them for the tamales, then take a couple of the extra husks and rip 24 strips ¼ inch (6 mm) wide and 8 inches long. Tie two together until you have 12 strips 15 to 16 inches (38 to 40 cm) long. You'll use these to tie the tamales.

✦ To assemble the tamales, grab a corn husk and place it in the palm of your hand. Use a spoon to add about ⅓ cup (91 g) of the dough to the center of the husk, leaving 1 inch (2.5 cm) free space on the top, left, and right sides and at least 3 to 4 inches (7.5 to 10 cm) of space on the bottom. The dough will expand as it cooks, so if you don't leave the inch of empty space for clearance at the top, it will ooze out.

(continues)

✦ Fold the right edge of the husk over the dough toward the left side, then take the left side of the husk and fold it over the right side to create a tube, then fold the bottom flap upward (leaving the top open). Tie a strip around the bottom of the tamal, to secure the bottom fold.

✦ As you work, place the folded tamales upright inside a steamer insert, making sure not to crowd the steamer insert.

✦ Add 1½ quarts (1.5 liters) water to a steamer pot. Add the steamer insert, cover, and bring the water to a boil (10 to 15 minutes). Reduce the heat to medium-low and steam for 1 hour 35 minutes to 1 hour 45 minutes. At the 1-hour mark, check the bottom of the pot for water and replenish as needed. If the water for the steam runs out, the bottom of the pot will burn and get ruined.

✦ It's tricky to tell when sweet tamales are done cooking because they're very soft while they're steaming but firm up once cooled; on average these tamales take 1 hour 40 minutes to fully cook. You can start checking for doneness at the 1 hour 25-minute mark. Simply take a tamal out and let it cool for 8 to 10 minutes, then check the inside. If the center looks a little raw or too soft, continue to let the tamales steam for another 10 to 20 minutes.

✦ Store in an airtight container or gallon-sized resealable plastic bag. These tamales will keep for 4 days max in the fridge, and 3 to 4 weeks in the freezer. The freshness and flavor start to decline past this. To reheat, steam for 20 to 30 minutes over medium-low heat until fully warmed through.

NOTE: This isn't necessary, but to ensure that no steam or condensation gets into each tamal, I like to take a second corn husk, wrap it around the top of the tamal, then fold down and tie it around the center to secure.

BEBIDAS

It's impossible to have pan dulce or tamales without a warm cup of café con leche, champurrado, or atole (or an ice-cold Coke, if you're my dad). In this chapter, you'll find a variety of drinks you can enjoy with pan dulce and desserts throughout the year, like my take on Maizena, a hot milk-based drink thickened with cornstarch that typically comes in premade packets with flavors like strawberry, coconut, vanilla, pecan, and chocolate. You'll also run into adult-friendly bevs, like my ponche de granada (pomegranate and hibiscus punch) or horchata rum punch. Both of these are perfect for a hot summer day but also come in handy if you're hosting during holidays because you can easily double the recipes for a large punch bowl. And I'm also sneaking in here a couple of aguas frescas (you have to try my melon basil agua fresca!) that you can have alongside any of the savory dishes and tamales in the Antojitos chapter.

DRINKS

Ponche navideño is essential during the holidays—how else are you going to wash down your tamales and buñue-los? This warm and aromatic punch is made with hibiscus and tamarind, sweetened with piloncillo, and packed with sugarcane and fruit like guavas and apples (and if you're an adult, a shot of tequila!).

PONCHE NAVIDEÑO
Mexican Christmas Punch

Makes about 12 cups (3 liters)

8 large tamarind pods, hard shell removed and strings pulled off (seeds should remain in the pods)

⅔ cup (32 g) dried hibiscus flowers

2 cinnamon sticks, broken in half

10 ounces (283 g) piloncillo, grated (or 1¼ cups/260 g brown sugar)

8 ounces (225 g) sugarcane, cut into 2- to 3-inch (5 to 7.5 cm) rectangles (see Tip)

1 cup (230 g) ripe tejocotes (Mexican hawthorn), sliced in half

6 small yellow guavas (about the size of a regular lime), quartered

1 green apple, halved and sliced thinly into half-moons

½ cup (105 g) prunes, pitted and roughly chopped

Tequila (optional)

✦ In a large stockpot, bring 12 cups (2.84 liters) water to a boil over medium heat. Add the tamarind, hibiscus, and cinnamon sticks, reduce the heat to medium-low, cover, and cook for 12 minutes. Use a slotted spoon to remove the cinnamon sticks and hibiscus flowers, then discard them. Optional: I also like to pull out the tamarind pulp and push it through a sieve (back into the pot) to strain out the seeds.

✦ Add the piloncillo, sugarcane, tejocotes, guavas, green apple, and prunes. Cover, set over low heat, and cook, stirring occasionally, until the fruit has softened, 25 to 30 minutes. Taste for sweetness and adjust as necessary.

✦ Use a ladle to pour the ponche into mugs, then serve warm with your favorite pan dulce. Add 2 ounces (60 g) of your favorite tequila to each mug for a more adult experience.

TIP: Unless you own a machete for cutting fresh sugarcane, it's easier to use the already peeled and packaged chunks you'll find in the freezer aisle or refrigerated section of your local grocery store!

Rompope is a Mexican milk and egg punch made with egg yolks, milk, sugar, and alcoholic spirits like rum or brandy. Quite a few Latin American countries have their own version of the drink, but Mexican rompope is said to originate from Puebla, Mexico, where the nuns from the Santa Clara convent took ponche de huevo from Spain and made it their own. I was never really a fan of rompope until I made it myself, and the addition of the hazelnut liqueur in my recipe is a welcome upgrade. The flavors in rompope will intensify as it sits, so I like to serve mine over ice after it's chilled in the refrigerator for at least 3 days. (If anything settles in the bottom, just give it a quick shake before serving.) Make an extra batch, as this is a great gift during the holidays!

ROMPOPE
Mexican Milk Punch

Makes 6 cups (1.4 liters)

3 cups (708 g) whole milk

2 large cinnamon sticks

¼ teaspoon freshly grated nutmeg

9 large egg yolks

1 (14-ounce/397 g) can sweetened condensed milk

2 teaspoons pure vanilla extract

Pinch of kosher salt

¾ cup (177 g) brandy or silver rum

⅓ cup (77 g) hazelnut liqueur

✦ In a medium saucepan, combine the milk, cinnamon sticks, and nutmeg. Let this mixture cook over low heat for 25 minutes, making sure the heat is at the absolute lowest setting or the milk will burn.

✦ While the milk is being infused, add the egg yolks to a large bowl and give them a whisk for a few seconds to break them up. After the milk has infused for 25 minutes, use a slotted spoon to remove the cinnamon sticks from the saucepan.

✦ While simultaneously whisking the egg yolks, pour a little bit of the hot milk mixture into the bowl to temper the yolks. Introducing a little bit of the hot liquid at a time while constantly whisking keeps the yolks from turning into scrambled eggs. After you've incorporated about ½ cup (118 g) of the hot milk, keep whisking the yolks and pour the rest of the hot milk mixture into the bowl in a slow and steady stream.

✦ Once all of the hot milk mixture and the yolks have been whisked together, whisk in the condensed milk, vanilla, salt, brandy, and hazelnut liqueur.

✦ Let the rompope cool completely before funneling it into a bottle, then refrigerate to chill. Serve over ice with a pinch of ground cinnamon and enjoy!

Champurrado is a chocolate-based atole, made with milk, Mexican chocolate, cinnamon, and nutmeg, then sweetened with piloncillo. When I was a kid, I used to look forward to Sundays because when we'd get out of Sunday school, street vendors would line up outside of church. I'd always run to get myself a warm cup of champurrado with a spicy tamal de pollo, and gelatina de mosaico in a plastic cup as a reward!

CHAMPURRADO

Makes about 8 cups (1.9 liters)

6½ cups (1.5 liters) whole milk

1 (12-ounce/340 g) can evaporated milk

1 teaspoon pure vanilla extract

2 sticks cinnamon

2 (3-ounce/90 g) tablets Mexican chocolate (like Ibarra or Abuelita)

½ cup plus 1 tablespoon (63 g) Maseca masa harina (for tortillas)

¼ cup (52 g) grated piloncillo or brown sugar

¼ teaspoon freshly grated nutmeg

✦ In a large stockpot or dutch oven, combine 5 cups (1.2 liters) of the whole milk, the evaporated milk, vanilla, and cinnamon sticks. Set the pot over just above low heat and cook for 30 minutes, whisking frequently to make sure nothing burns or sticks to the pan.

✦ Meanwhile, grate the chocolate discs on the large holes of a box grater into a large bowl. Add the masa harina, piloncillo, and nutmeg, then whisk in the remaining 1½ cups (355 g) milk.

✦ Whisk the chocolate/masa harina mixture into the hot milk mixture, then bump up the heat to medium-low and cook, still whisking frequently, until it starts to thicken, another 10 to 12 minutes.

✦ Taste the champurrado and see if it needs any more sugar and add accordingly. Remove the cinnamon sticks with a pair of tongs. Serve in mugs with pan dulce on the side.

This ponche de granada is inspired by the ponche my dad brings back from his trips to Mexico (and stashes in the refrigerator until the holidays come around) made with hibiscus tea, pomegranate juice, and cane alcohol. If you happen to visit the city of Colima, head out to the town of Comala and grab a bottle of ponche from Don Tavo; they make the best ponche de nuez, cajeta, and granada!

PONCHE DE GRANADA
Pomegranate Punch

Makes about 6 cups (1.4 liters)

1½ cups (72 g) dried hibiscus flowers

⅓ cup (67 g) granulated sugar

1¼ cups (295 g) pomegranate juice

Juice of 1 lime

1 cup (236 g) vodka

½ cup (85 g) pomegranate arils

Ice, for serving

✦ In a medium saucepan, bring 4 cups (1 liter) water to a boil. Reduce to a simmer, add the hibiscus, and cook for 6 minutes. Remove from the heat, then use a slotted spoon to remove the hibiscus. Stir in the sugar and let the mixture cool to room temperature. Strain into a container, then transfer to the refrigerator to cool completely.

✦ To make the punch, in a pitcher, stir together the chilled hibiscus tea, pomegranate juice, lime juice, vodka, and pomegranate arils. Taste for sugar and adjust if necessary. Serve over ice.

Typically enjoyed when the weather is cold, atole is an accompaniment for pan dulce or tamales. Although this drink is made in a variety of different flavors—like pineapple, strawberry, and vanilla—coconut is my favorite of the bunch because of the creaminess that the coconut fat adds to the drink.

COCONUT ATOLE

Makes about 10 cups (2.4 liters)

½ cup plus 1 tablespoon
  (63 g) Maseca masa harina
  (for tortillas)

2 cups (472 g) whole milk

4 (13.5-ounce/398 g) cans
  full-fat coconut milk

1 teaspoon pure vanilla extract

1 (14-ounce/397 g) can
  sweetened condensed milk

✦ In a medium bowl, whisk together the masa harina and whole milk. Set aside.

✦ In a large stockpot or dutch oven, whisk together the coconut milk, vanilla, and condensed milk and bring to a simmer over medium heat, 8 to 10 minutes.

✦ Whisk in the masa harina slurry, then reduce the heat to medium-low and cook until it starts to thicken, 10 to 12 minutes.

✦ Serve hot.

Maizena is a brand of a hot, milk-based drink that is similar to atole, but instead of being thickened with corn flour, it's thickened with cornstarch. The ready-made pouches of mix come in flavors like vanilla, pecan, strawberry, and chocolate, but by making the drink from scratch you can pack it with even more flavor. Maizena de vainilla (vanilla) and nuez (pecan) are my favorites, because those are the flavors my mom made the most!

MAIZENA DE VAINILLA AND MAIZENA DE NUEZ

Each makes about 8 cups (1.9 liters)

FOR THE MAIZENA DE VAINILLA
1½ cups (354 g) cold water

½ cup (64 g) cornstarch

6 cups (1.4 liters) whole milk

1 (14-ounce/397 g) can sweetened condensed milk

2 teaspoons pure vanilla extract

1 stick cinnamon

FOR THE MAIZENA DE NUEZ
¾ cup (177 g) cold water

⅓ cup (37 g) cornstarch

1 cup (106 g) chopped pecans

6 cups (1.4 liters) whole milk

1 (14-ounce/397 g) can sweetened condensed milk

1 teaspoon pure vanilla extract

+ **Make the Maizena de vainilla:** In a measuring cup, whisk together the cold water and cornstarch. Set aside.

+ In a large stockpot or dutch oven, whisk together the whole milk, condensed milk, and vanilla. Add the cinnamon stick. Bring to a simmer over medium heat, 8 to 10 minutes. Whisk in the cornstarch slurry, making sure you're whisking rapidly so the cornstarch mixture doesn't clump up. Reduce the heat to medium-low and cook until the mixture starts to thicken, 8 to 10 minutes.

+ Serve hot.

+ **Make the Maizena de nuez:** In a small bowl, whisk together the cold water and cornstarch. Set aside.

+ In a large skillet, toast the chopped pecans over medium-low heat until nice and fragrant, 4 to 5 minutes. Remove from the heat and transfer them to a blender. Add 2 cups (472 g) of the whole milk and blend until smooth, 45 seconds to 1 minute.

+ Strain this mixture into a large stockpot or dutch oven, then stir in the remaining 4 cups (944 g) whole milk. Whisk in the condensed milk and vanilla and bring to a simmer over medium heat, 8 to 10 minutes.

+ As soon as it reaches a simmer, reduce the heat to medium-low and whisk in the cornstarch slurry. Cook until it starts to thicken, 9 to 10 minutes longer.

+ Serve hot.

Most days before we left for school, my mom would prep us with a cup of chocolate caliente (hot chocolate) with a warm bolillo sliced in half with a dab of butter and a sprinkle of sugar. This was a warm and comforting treat, and it kept our bellies full. Chocolate en agua (see Variation below) is similar to hot chocolate, just made with water rather than milk.

CHOCOLATE CALIENTE

Serves 4

4½ cups (1 liter) whole milk

1 tablet (90 g) Mexican chocolate, grated

½ teaspoon pure vanilla extract

½ cinnamon stick

✦ In a large stockpot or dutch oven, whisk together the milk and grated chocolate. Stir in the vanilla, and add the cinnamon stick. Bring the mixture to a simmer over medium-low heat, 12 to 15 minutes. Remove the cinnamon stick and serve hot.

Variation

CHOCOLATE EN AGUA: Replace the milk with 4 cups (950 g) water. Increase the cinnamon sticks to 2. The rest of the recipe is the same.

Café de olla is coffee that is traditionally made in an olla de barro (clay pot) with aromatics like cinnamon, orange peel, and cloves, then sweetened with piloncillo. However, when I am craving a hot cup of café de olla, I make it *sin* olla. My method of choice is a French press, but if you're more into the pour over or drip coffee maker, you can still make this. For an 8- to 12-cup (2- to 2.3-liter) drip coffee maker or pour over, add ¼ teaspoon ground cinnamon, ½ teaspoon grated orange zest, and a tiny pinch of ground cloves on top of the ground coffee in the basket. Continue to prepare the coffee as you normally would and pour over the sugar in the coffee mug to serve.

CAFÉ SIN OLLA

Serves 2 or 3

½ cup (33 g) coarsely ground medium- or dark-roast coffee

1 stick cinnamon

1 strip orange zest, 3 inches (7.5 cm) long and ½ inch (1.25 cm) wide

2 whole cloves

Dark brown sugar or grated piloncillo

✦ In an 8-cup (34-fluid ounce/1-liter) French press, combine the coffee, cinnamon stick, orange zest, and cloves.

✦ Bring 4 cups (944 g) water to a boil in an electric kettle or on the stove. Once it boils, remove it from the heat and let it sit for 2 minutes to cool down just enough to reach an optimal coffee-brewing temperature.

✦ Pour the water over the coffee in the French press, then give it a stir and place the lid with the plunger on top to hold in the heat. Let the press sit like this for 5 minutes, then carefully push the plunger all the way down.

✦ To serve, place 1 to 2 teaspoons sugar in the bottom of a coffee mug and pour in the hot coffee. Stir and adjust the sugar to taste.

Hibiscus and cherry go together like peanut butter and jelly. The tartness from the hibiscus tea complements and balances the sweetness from the dark cherries—and makes for an agua fresca with great depth of flavor!

CHERRY HIBISCUS AGUA FRESCA

Makes about 8 cups (1.9 liters)

1 cup (48 g) dried hibiscus flowers

1 pound (455 g) dark sweet cherries (about 2 cups), fresh or thawed frozen, pitted

¾ cup (150 g) granulated sugar

½ cup (118 g) fresh lime juice (from about 4 limes)

Ice, for serving

✦ In a small saucepan, bring 3 cups (708 g) water to a boil over medium heat. Stir in the hibiscus flowers, reduce the heat to medium-low, and let cook for 5 minutes. Remove from the heat. Use a slotted spoon to remove the hibiscus flowers, then let the hibiscus tea cool completely.

✦ In a blender, combine the cherries and 3½ cups (826 g) water and blend on medium-high speed until completely smooth, about 1 minute.

✦ Strain this mixture into a large pitcher. Stir in the cooled hibiscus tea, the sugar, and lime juice. Refrigerate for 2 hours to chill and serve over ice.

I love citrus, so it's no surprise that agua de limón con chia is my all-time favorite agua fresca. This is essentially a limeade made with freshly squeezed lime juice and water, then sweetened with sugar. In Mexico, street vendors stir chia seeds into it. Why? There's no real answer—it's just tradition!

LIME CHIA AGUA FRESCA

Makes about 8 cups (1.9 liters)

¾ cup (177 g) fresh lime juice (from 6 to 7 limes)

½ cup (100 g) granulated sugar, plus more to taste

1 tablespoon chia seeds

Ice, for serving

→ In a large pitcher, stir together 7¼ cups (1.7 liters) water, the lime juice, and sugar. Taste for sugar, adjust, then stir in the chia seeds. Refrigerate for
2 hours to chill. Serve over ice.

There's something about the combination of sweet cantaloupe, aromatic basil, and fresh lemon juice that makes this cantaloupe basil agua fresca taste like a hot summer day in Italy. It's soo good, and a shot of vodka or tequila would make it even better! I'm also including a recipe for traditional agua de melon (cantaloupe agua fresca) for those days when you're just looking for a good classic. You can easily halve the agua de melon recipe and add some extra sugar (and some diced cantaloupe as well) for quick and easy paletas de melon.

AGUAS DE MELON
Cantaloupe Aguas Frescas

Makes about 8 cups (1.9 liters)

FOR THE CANTELOUPE BASIL AGUA FRESCA

2 cups (10 ounces/285 g) cubed cantaloupe

2 cups (10 ounces/285 g) cubed seedless watermelon

½ cup (118 g) fresh lemon juice (4 to 5 medium lemons)

6 large fresh basil leaves

⅓ cup (112 g) honey, plus more to taste

Ice, for serving

FOR THE AGUA DE MELON

6 cups (1 pound 14 ounces/ 850 g) cubed cantaloupe (from 1 medium cantaloupe)

¼ cup (50 g) granulated sugar

Juice of ½ lime

Ice, for serving

✦ **Make the cantaloupe basil agua fresca:** In a blender, combine the cantaloupe, watermelon, lemon juice, basil leaves, honey, and 4 cups (944 g) water and blend on medium-high speed until smooth, 45 seconds to 1 minute. Strain the mixture through a sieve into a large pitcher, making sure not to press too much of the pulp through, then whisk in 2 cups (472 g) water. Refrigerate for at least 2 hours to chill. Serve over ice.

✦ **Make the agua de melon:** In a blender, combine the cantaloupe and 4 cups (944 g) water and blend on medium-high speed until smooth, 45 seconds to 1 minute. Strain through a sieve into a large pitcher, making sure not to press too much of the pulp through, then stir in 2 cups (472 g) water, the sugar, and lime juice. Refrigerate for at least 2 hours to chill. Serve over ice.

When I was growing up, agua de pepino was regularly in our refrigerator. It was one of my dad's favorites! The combination of cucumber and lime makes it refreshing, which is so good during the summer, but this drink also pairs perfectly with rich saucy dishes, like Enfrijoladas (page 166).

CUCUMBER LIME AGUA FRESCA

Makes about 8 cups (1.9 liters)

2 large cucumbers, peeled and
    seeded, roughly chopped into
    large chunks
⅔ cup (157 g) fresh lime juice
    (from 6 to 7 limes)
½ cup (100 g) granulated sugar
Ice, for serving

✦ In a blender, combine the cucumbers and 4 cups (944 g) water and blend on medium-high speed until smooth, 45 seconds to 1 minute. Gently strain the mixture through a sieve into a large pitcher, making sure not to push all of the pulp through. Stir in 2 cups (472 g) water, the lime juice, and sugar. Refrigerate for 2 hours to chill. Serve over ice.

When the holidays come around, I like to have a few drink recipes up my sleeve so I don't have to play bartender all night. This horchata rum punch has a milky cinnamon horchata base sweetened with condensed milk and a nutty layer from the hazelnut liqueur. It's become one of my favorite big-batch cocktails to make year-round.

HORCHATA RUM PUNCH

Makes about 8 cups (1.9 liters)

½ cup (55g) sliced almonds

1½ Mexican cinnamon sticks (4 inches/10 cm), broken in half

1 cup (175 g) long-grain white rice

3½ cups (826 g) hot (not boiling) water

3 cups (708 g) cold water

1 (14-ounce/397 g) can sweetened condensed milk

1 teaspoon pure vanilla extract

⅔ cup (157 g) hazelnut liqueur

¾ cup (177 g) silver rum

Ice, for serving

Ground cinnamon, for serving

+ In a dry skillet, toast the almonds and broken cinnamon sticks over medium-low heat, stirring occasionally to make sure the almonds don't burn, just until the almonds start to turn golden brown and fragrant, 4 to 5 minutes. (You don't want to completely toast them or they'll overpower the flavor.) Remove from the heat.

+ In a large bowl, mix together the rice, almonds, and cinnamon sticks, then pour in the hot water. Make sure the water is hot to the touch but isn't boiling, as you don't want to cook the rice. Set aside and let rest for 4 to 6 hours.

+ Pour the mixture (liquid and all) into a blender and blend for 30 seconds, then strain through a coffee filter (to ensure your horchata isn't chalky or grainy) into a pitcher. Stir in the cold water, condensed milk, vanilla, hazelnut liqueur, and rum. Refrigerate for 2 hours to chill. Serve over ice with a sprinkle of ground cinnamon.

ACKNOWLEDGMENTS

To my husband, Billy:

For the past twelve years, you've shown me exactly what unconditional love and support is, and I just want you to know that I appreciate you so much. Whether it is going on grocery trips for me, helping me test and develop recipes when I'm stretched thin, or just making me laugh when I'm stressed and having a rough day, I can always count on you.

Like two young saplings that grow together, may you find solace in my leafy canopy. :)

I love you!

To my agent, Dado:

Dado, I know I tell you this every time we talk, but I really appreciate you and everything you've done for me! Thank you, thank you, thank you for helping me bring this book to life. You are the best!

To my editor, Elizabeth Smith:

Thank you so much for making the book writing process so smooth. I really enjoyed getting to work together on this book!

To my publishing team at Harper Design:

I couldn't have asked for a better team—thank you all for your hard work!

INDEX

agave nectar, in Tamales de Fresa (Sweet Strawberry Tamales), 183–84

aguas frescas, *see* bebidas (drinks)

almonds, in Horchata Rum Punch, 213

antojitos (bites), 159–85
  Crema de Frijol con Chochoyotes, 170
  Enfrijoladas, 166
  Molletes, 178
  Picaditas, 169
  see also tamales

apples
  Caramel Apple Cheesecake Empanadas, 97–98
  Ponche Navideño (Mexican Christmas Punch), 188

Arroz con Leche, 108

basil, in Cantaloupe Basil Agua Fresca, 208

beans or refried beans
  Crema de Frijol con Chochoyotes, 170
  Enfrijoladas, 166
  Molletes, 178

bebidas (drinks), 187–213
  Aguas de Melon (Cantaloupe Aguas Frescas), 208
  Café sin Olla, 203
  Champurrado, 192
  Cherry Hibiscus Agua Fresca, 204
  Chocolate Caliente, 200
  Coconut Atole, 196
  Cucumber Lime Agua Fresca, 210
  Horchata Rum Punch, 213
  Lime Chia Agua Fresca, 207
  Maizena de Nuez, 199

Maizena de Vainilla, 199
  Ponche de Granada (Pomegranate Punch), 195
  Ponche Navideño (Mexican Christmas Punch), 188
  Rompope (Mexican Milk Punch), 191

beef, in Tamales de Res con Chile Rojo (Red Beef æTamales), 160–62

bell peppers
  Crema de Frijol con Chochoyotes, 170
  Enfrijoladas, 166

Berry Hibiscus Danishes, 125–27

Besitos de Nuez (Mexican Wedding Cookies), 56–58

Bolillos (Bolillo Rolls), 29–30
  in Molletes, 178

bourbon
  Cajeta Envinada (Cinnamon Rum Cajeta Sauce), 36
  Vanilla Extract (recipe), 38
  Volteado de Piña (Fresh Pineapple Upside-Down Cake), 77–79

brandy, in Rompope (Mexican Milk Punch), 191

Brownies, Dulce de Leche, 94–96

Buñuelos de Viento, 90

butter, 17
  Honey Butter, 70

buttermilk, *see* milk and buttermilk

Café con Leche Flan, 118

Café sin Olla, 203

cajeta, 17
  Cajeta Envinada (Cinnamon Rum Cajeta Sauce), 36
  Classic Chocoflan, 130–32

Dulce de Leche Brownies, 94–96
  Spiced Pumpkin Chocoflan, 153–54

cakes and loaves
  Carlota de Mango Con Limón, 149
  Chicano Eats Birthday Cake, 145–46
  Classic Carrot Cake, 150
  Classic Chocoflan, 130–32
  Cortadillo (Mexican Pink Cake), 59–60
  Horchata Sheet Cake, 139–40
  Horchata Tiramisu, 111–12
  Niño Envuelto, 87–89
  Pan de Elote, 73
  Panque de Nuez (Sweet Pecan Loaf), 69
  Rebanadas, 70
  Red Velvet Chocoflan, 143–44
  Rosca de Reyes (King's Cake), 84–86
  Spiced Pumpkin Chocoflan, 153–54
  Tres Leches, 136–38
  Volteado de Piña (Fresh Pineapple Upside-Down Cake), 77–79

cantaloupe
  Agua de Melon (Cantaloupe Agua Fresca), 208
  Cantaloupe Basil Agua Fresca, 208

Caramel Apple Cheesecake Empanadas, 97–98

Carlota de Mango Con Limón, 149

carrots, in Classic Carrot Cake, 150

Champurrado, 192

Cheesecake, Churro, 133–35

Cherry Hibiscus Agua Fresca, 204
chia seeds, in Lime Chia Agua
    Fresca, 207
Chicano Eats Birthday Cake,
    145–46
The Chicano Eats Chocolate Chip
    Cookie, 102–4
chicken, in Tamales de Chile
    Verde con Pollo (Chicken
    Chile Verde Tamales),
    172–74
chile peppers
    Crema de Frijol con
        Chochoyotes, 170
    Enfrijoladas, 166
    Molletes, 178
    Picaditas, 169
    Tamales de Chile Verde con
        Pollo (Chicken Chile
        Verde Tamales), 172–74
    Tamales de Rajas con
        Queso (Rajas con Queso
        Tamales), 175–77
    Tamales de Res con Chile
        Rojo (Red Beef Tamales),
        160–62
Chochoyotes, Crema de Frijol
    con, 170
chocolate
    Buttercream Frosting,
        145–46
    Champurrado, 192
    Chicano Eats Birthday Cake,
        145–46
    The Chicano Eats Chocolate
        Chip Cookie, 102–4
    Chocolate Caliente, 200
    Classic Chocoflan, 130–32
    Dulce de Leche Brownies,
        94–96
    Hibiscus and White
        Chocolate Oatmeal
        Cookies, 122–24
    Horchata Tiramisu, 111–12
    Polvorones Tricolor
        (Tricolored Sugar
        Cookies), 62
    Red Velvet Chocoflan,
        143–44

Spiced Pumpkin Chocoflan,
    153–54
    see also white chocolate
chorizo or longaniza
    Crema de Frijol con
        Chochoyotes, 170
    Enfrijoladas, 166
    Molletes, 178
Churro Cheesecake, 133–35
cilantro
    Crema de Frijol con
        Chochoyotes, 170
    Molletes, 178
    Tamales de Chile Verde con
        Pollo (Chicken Chile
        Verde Tamales), 172–74
    Tamales de Rajas con
        Queso (Rajas con Queso
        Tamales), 175–77
cinnamon
    Arroz con Leche, 108
    Buñuelos de Viento, 90
    Café sin Olla, 203
    Cajeta Envinada (Cinnamon
        Rum Cajeta Sauce), 36
    Caramel Apple Cheesecake
        Empanadas, 97–98
    Champurrado, 192
    Chocolate Caliente, 200
    Classic Carrot Cake, 150
    Horchata Rum Punch, 213
    Horchata Tiramisu, 111–12
    Maizena de Vainilla, 199
    Ponche Navideño (Mexican
        Christmas Punch), 188
    Roles de Canela (Cinnamon
        Rolls), 47–50
    Rompope (Mexican Milk
        Punch), 191
Classic Caramel Flan, 101
Classic Carrot Cake, 150
Classic Chocoflan, 130–32
Classic Vanilla Bean Cream
    Cheese Icing, 51
coconut, in Niño Envuelto, 87–89
coconut milk
    Coconut Atole, 196
    Dairy-Free Coconut
        Caramel Sauce, 32

coffee liqueur, in Horchata
    Tiramisu, 111–12
coffee or espresso
    Café con Leche Flan, 118
    Café sin Olla, 203
    Classic Chocoflan, 130–32
    Horchata Tiramisu, 111–12
Conchas (Vanilla Conchas),
    44–46
condensed milk, 17
    Arroz con Leche, 108
    Café con Leche Flan, 118
    Carlota de Mango Con
        Limón, 149
    Classic Caramel Flan, 101
    Classic Chocoflan,
        130–32
    Coconut Atole, 196
    Horchata Rum Punch, 213
    Maizena de Nuez, 199
    Maizena de Vainilla, 199
    Pan de Elote, 73
    Pay de Limón con Coco
        (Coconut Key Lime Pie),
        113–14
    Red Velvet Chocoflan,
        143–44
    Rompope (Mexican Milk
        Punch), 191
    Spiced Pumpkin Chocoflan,
        153–54
    Strawberries and Cream
        Gelatina, 117
    Tres Leches, 136–38
cookies/bars
    Besitos de Nuez (Mexican
        Wedding Cookies), 56–58
    The Chicano Eats Chocolate
        Chip Cookie, 102–4
    Dulce de Leche Brownies,
        94–96
    Galletas Grageas (Mexican
        Sprinkle Cookies), 66
    Hibiscus and White
        Chocolate Oatmeal
        Cookies, 122–24
    Marranitos (Mexican
        Gingerbread Pig
        Cookies), 55

No-Bake Cookies and
Cream Cheesecake Bars,
155–57
Polvorones Rosas (Pink
Sugar Cookies), 65
Polvorones Tricolor
(Tricolored Sugar
Cookies), 62
Strawberry Guava
Shortbread Bars, 105–7
corn
Pan de Elote, 73
Tamales de Elote (Sweet
Corn Tamales), 163–65
corn flour, *see* masa harina
corn husks, *see* Tamales
Cortadillo (Mexican Pink Cake),
59–60
cream
Carlota de Mango Con
Limón, 149
Crema Batida (Whipped
Cream), 35, 138
Horchata Tiramisu, 111–12
No-Bake Cookies and
Cream Cheesecake Bars,
155–57
Pay de Limón con Coco
(Coconut Key Lime Pie),
113–14
Tres Leches, 136–38
cream cheese
Berry Hibiscus Danishes,
125–27
Caramel Apple Cheesecake
Empanadas, 97–98
Carlota de Mango Con
Limón, 149
Churro Cheesecake,
133–35
Classic Carrot Cake, 150
Classic Chocoflan,
130–32
Classic Vanilla Bean Cream
Cheese Icing, 51
and Dulce de Leche
Pinwheels, 121
Fluffy Dulce de Leche
Frosting, 51

No-Bake Cookies and
Cream Cheesecake Bars,
155–57
Pastelitos de Guayaba, 80
Red Velvet Chocoflan,
143–44
Spiced Pumpkin Chocoflan,
153–54
Strawberries and Cream
Gelatina, 117
cream of coconut, in Pay de
Limón con Coco (Coconut
Key Lime Pie), 113–14
Crema Batida (Whipped Cream),
35, 138
Crema de Frijol con
Chochoyotes, 170
crema Mexicana cheese
Crema de Frijol con
Chochoyotes, 170
Picaditas, 169
Cucumber Lime Agua Fresca,
210

Dairy-Free Coconut Caramel
Sauce, 32
dulce de leche, 17
Caramel Apple Cheesecake
Empanadas, 97–98
Classic Chocoflan, 130–32
Cream Cheese and Dulce de
Leche Pinwheels, 121
Dulce de Leche (recipe), 41
Dulce de Leche Brownies,
94–96
Fluffy Dulce de Leche
Frosting, 51
Niño Envuelto, 87–89
Spiced Pumpkin Chocoflan,
153–54

eggs, 17
Café con Leche Flan, 118
Classic Caramel Flan, 101
Classic Chocoflan, 130–32
Horchata Tiramisu, 111–12
Pan de Muerto, 74–76

Pay de Limón con Coco
(Coconut Key Lime Pie),
113–14
Red Velvet Chocoflan,
143–44
Rompope (Mexican Milk
Punch), 191
Spiced Pumpkin Chocoflan,
153–54
Tres Leches, 136–38
Empanadas, Caramel Apple
Cheesecake, 97–98
Enfrijoladas, 166
evaporated milk
Champurrado, 192
Classic Chocoflan, 130–32
Tres Leches, 136–38

flan and flan desserts
Café con Leche Flan, 118
Classic Caramel Flan, 101
Classic Chocoflan, 130–32
Red Velvet Chocoflan,
143–44
Spiced Pumpkin Chocoflan,
153–54
Fluffy Dulce de Leche Frosting,
51
fritters, Buñuelos de Viento, 90
frostings and icings
Chocolate Buttercream,
145–46
Classic Vanilla Bean Cream
Cheese Icing, 51
Cream Cheese Frosting, 150
Fluffy Dulce de Leche Frosting, 51
Vanilla Buttercream, 59–60,
139–40

Galletas Grageas (Mexican
Sprinkle Cookies), 66
Gelatina, Strawberries and
Cream, 117
guava paste, 17
Pastelitos de Guayaba, 80
Strawberry Guava
Shortbread Bars, 105–7

guavas, in Ponche Navideño (Mexican Christmas Punch), 188

half-and-half
    Café con Leche Flan, 118
    Classic Caramel Flan, 101
    Red Velvet Chocoflan, 143–44
    Spiced Pumpkin Chocoflan, 153–54
hazelnut liqueur
    Besitos de Nuez (Mexican Wedding Cookies), 56–58
    Crema Batida (Whipped Cream), 35
    Horchata Rum Punch, 213
    Horchata Tiramisu, 111–12
    Rompope (Mexican Milk Punch), 191
    Tres Leches, 136–38
hibiscus flowers
    Berry Hibiscus Danishes, 125–27
    Cherry Hibiscus Agua Fresca, 204
    Hibiscus and White Chocolate Oatmeal Cookies, 122–24
    Ponche de Granada (Pomegranate Punch), 195
    Ponche Navideño (Mexican Christmas Punch), 188
    Tamales de Fresa (Sweet Strawberry Tamales), 183–84
honey
    Cantaloupe Basil Agua Fresca, 208
    Rebanadas, 70
    Tamales de Elote (Sweet Corn Tamales), 163–65
    Tamales de Fresa (Sweet Strawberry Tamales), 183–84

Tamales de Piña (Sweet Pineapple Tamales), 181–82
horchata
    Horchata Cream, 112
    Horchata Rum Punch, 213
    Horchata Sheet Cake, 139–40
    Horchata Tiramisu, 111–12

icings, see frostings and icings

kitchen tools, 18–19
    comals, 18, 23, 24
    double boilers, 94, 157
    scales, 19, 20, 21
    steamer pots, 162, 165, 177, 181–82, 184
    thermometers, 19, 21
    tortilla presses, 19, 23, 169
    tortilla warmers, 19, 24

ladyfingers, in Carlota de Mango Con Limón, 149
lemons/lemon juice
    Cantaloupe Basil Agua Fresca, 208
    Strawberries and Cream Gelatina, 117
limes/lime juice
    Agua de Melon (Cantaloupe Agua Fresca), 208
    Berry Hibiscus Danishes, 125–27
    Carlota de Mango Con Limón, 149
    Cherry Hibiscus Agua Fresca, 204
    Cucumber Lime Agua Fresca, 210
    Lime Chia Agua Fresca, 207
    Pastelitos de Guayaba, 80
    Pay de Limón con Coco (Coconut Key Lime Pie), 113–14
    Ponche de Granada (Pomegranate Punch), 195

Strawberries and Cream Gelatina, 117

Maizena de Nuez, 199
Maizena de Vainilla, 199
mangos, in Carlota de Mango Con Limón, 149
Mantecadas (Sweet Muffins), 52
Marranitos (Mexican Gingerbread Pig Cookies), 55
masa harina, 17
    Champurrado, 192
    Coconut Atole, 196
    Crema de Frijol con Chochoyotes, 170
    Picaditas, 169
    in tamales, see Tamales
    Tortillas de Maíz (Corn Tortillas), 23
mascarpone cheese, in Horchata Tiramisu, 111–12
milk and buttermilk, 18
    Arroz con Leche, 108
    Chocolate Caliente, 200
    Coconut Atole, 196
    Dulce de Leche (recipe), 41
    Horchata Sheet Cake, 139–40
    Red Velvet Chocoflan, 143–44
    Strawberries and Cream Gelatina, 117
    Tres Leches, 136–38
    see also condensed milk; evaporated milk
molasses, in Marranitos (Mexican Gingerbread Pig Cookies), 55
Molletes, 178
mozzarella cheese
    Enfrijoladas, 166
    Molletes, 178
    Tamales de Rajas con Queso (Rajas con Queso Tamales), 175–77
muffins, Mantecadas (Sweet Muffins), 52

Niño Envuelto, 87–89
No-Bake Cookies and Cream Cheesecake Bars, 155–57

oats, in Hibiscus and White Chocolate Oatmeal Cookies, 122–24
Oaxaca cheese, in Enfrijoladas, 166
oranges
    Café sin Olla, 203
    Pan de Muerto, 74–76
Orejitas, 83

Pan de Elote, 73
Pan de Muerto, 74–76
panela cheese, in Tamales de Rajas con Queso (Rajas con Queso Tamales), 175–77
Panque de Nuez (Sweet Pecan Loaf), 69
pantry staples, 17–18
Pastelitos de Guayaba, 80
Pay de Limón con Coco (Coconut Key Lime Pie), 113–14
pecans
    Besitos de Nuez (Mexican Wedding Cookies), 56–58
    Maizena de Nuez, 199
    Panque de Nuez (Sweet Pecan Loaf), 69
peppers, see bell peppers; chile peppers
Picaditas, 169
Pico de Gallo, 178
piloncillo
    Champurrado, 192
    Ponche Navideño (Mexican Christmas Punch), 188
pineapple
    Tamales de Piña (Sweet Pineapple Tamales), 181–82
    Volteado de Piña (Fresh Pineapple Upside-Down Cake), 77–79

Polvorones Rosas (Pink Sugar Cookies), 65
Polvorones Tricolor (Tricolored Sugar Cookies), 62
pomegranates, in Ponche de Granada (Pomegranate Punch), 195
Ponche de Granada (Pomegranate Punch), 195
Ponche Navideño (Mexican Christmas Punch), 188
prunes, in Ponche Navideño (Mexican Christmas Punch), 188
puff pastry, 18
    Berry Hibiscus Danishes, 125–27
    Cream Cheese and Dulce de Leche Pinwheels, 121
    Orejitas, 83
    Pastelitos de Guayaba, 80
pumpkin, in Spiced Pumpkin Chocoflan, 153–54

Rebanadas, 70
Red Velvet Chocoflan, 143–44
rice
    Arroz con Leche, 108
    Horchata Rum Punch, 213
Roles de Canela (Cinnamon Rolls), 47–50
Rompope (Mexican Milk Punch), 191
Rosca de Reyes (King's Cake), 84–86
rum
    Cajeta Envinada (Cinnamon Rum Cajeta Sauce), 36
    Horchata Rum Punch, 213
    Horchata Tiramisu, 111–12
    Rompope (Mexican Milk Punch), 191
    Volteado de Piña (Fresh Pineapple Upside-Down Cake), 77–79

sauces and toppings
    cajeta, see cajeta
    Crema Batida (Whipped Cream), 35, 138
    Dairy-Free Coconut Caramel Sauce, 32
    dulce de leche, see dulce de leche
    frostings and icings, see frostings and icings
    Honey Butter, 70
    Pico de Gallo, 178
    Salsa Roja (Red Salsa), 169
    Salsa Verde (Green Salsa), 175
scales, 19, 20, 21
shortening, 18
sopes, in Picaditas, 169
soups, Crema de Frijol con Chochoyotes, 170
sour cream
    Churro Cheesecake, 133–35
    Crema Batida (Whipped Cream), 35, 138
    Pay de Limón con Coco (Coconut Key Lime Pie), 113–14
    Strawberry Guava Shortbread Bars, 105–7
    Tres Leches, 136–38
strawberries
    Strawberries and Cream Gelatina, 117
    Strawberry Guava Shortbread Bars, 105–7
    Tamales de Fresa (Sweet Strawberry Tamales), 183–84
sugarcane, in Ponche Navideño (Mexican Christmas Punch), 188

Tamales
    de Chile Verde con Pollo (Chicken Chile Verde Tamales), 172–74
    de Elote (Sweet Corn Tamales), 163–65

de Fresa (Sweet Strawberry Tamales), 183–84

de Piña (Sweet Pineapple Tamales), 181–82

de Rajas con Queso (Rajas con Queso Tamales), 175–77

de Res con Chile Rojo (Red Beef Tamales), 160–62

tamarind pods, in Ponche Navideño (Mexican Christmas Punch), 188

tejocotes (Mexican hawthorn), in Ponche Navideño (Mexican Christmas Punch), 188

Teleras (Telera Rolls), 27–28
in Molletes, 178

tequila, in Ponche Navideño (Mexican Christmas Punch), 188

tips/notes, 17–21
butter, 107
clear vanilla extract, 60
coffee or espresso, 112
cookies/bars, 104, 124
flan and flan desserts, 144, 154
flour tortillas, 24
gel food coloring, 46
kitchen tools, see kitchen tools
masa harina, 23
mise en place, 21
pantry staples, 17–18
pineapple, 79
puff pastry, 80, 83
tamales, 165, 182, 184
video basics, 21
weight equivalents, 20
whipped cream, 114

Tiramisu, Horchata, 111–12

tomatillos
Salsa Verde (Green Salsa), 175
Tamales de Chile Verde con Pollo (Chicken Chile Verde Tamales), 172–74

Tamales de Rajas con Queso (Rajas con Queso Tamales), 175–77

tomatoes
Molletes, 178
Picaditas, 169
Pico de Gallo, 178
Salsa Roja (Red Salsa), 169

tools, see kitchen tools

toppings, see sauces and toppings

tortillas
Enfrijoladas, 166
Tortillas de Harina (Flour Tortillas), 24
Tortillas de Maíz (Corn Tortillas), 23

Tres Leches, 136–38

vanilla extract/paste, 18
Arroz con Leche, 108
Berry Hibiscus Danishes, 125–27
Buttercream Frosting, 59–60, 139–40
Café con Leche Flan, 118
Classic Caramel Flan, 101
Classic Carrot Cake, 150
Classic Vanilla Bean Cream Cheese Icing, 51
Conchas (Vanilla Conchas), 44–46
Cortadillo (Mexican Pink Cake), 59–60
Dulce de Leche, 41
Horchata Rum Punch, 213
Maizena de Nuez, 199
Maizena de Vainilla, 199
Mantecadas (Sweet Muffins), 52
Pan de Elote, 73
Rompope (Mexican Milk Punch), 191
Tres Leches, 136–38
Vanilla Extract (recipe), 38

vodka
Ponche de Granada (Pomegranate Punch), 195
Vanilla Extract (recipe), 38

Volteado de Piña (Fresh Pineapple Upside-Down Cake), 77–79

walnuts, in Classic Carrot Cake, 150

watermelon, in Cantaloupe Basil Agua Fresca, 208

white chocolate
Hibiscus and White Chocolate Oatmeal Cookies, 122–24
No-Bake Cookies and Cream Cheesecake Bars, 155–57

yeast breads/sweet rolls
Bolillos (Bolillo Rolls), 29–30
Conchas (Vanilla Conchas), 44–46
Pan de Muerto, 74–76
Rebanadas, 70
Roles de Canela (Cinnamon Rolls), 47–50
Rosca de Reyes (King's Cake), 84–86
Teleras (Telera Rolls), 27–28

ABOUT THE AUTHOR

Esteban Castillo is a recipe developer, food photographer, and the author of the award-winning food blog and best-selling book *Chicano Eats* and was the 2017 Saveur Blog Awards winner for Best New Voice. He lives in Fresno, California, with his husband, Billy, and their three dogs, Nomi, Rigby, and Jepsen.